Practise your Conjunctions and Linkers

Donald Adamson

Series editor: Donald Adamson

Contents

Introduction

This book aims to help learners with the conjunctions, adverbs and prepositions which are used to link stretches of language. These are often referred to as LINKERS.

Linkers are important in every situation where students have to organise and present their ideas. Indeed, work on linkers may well have a 'spin-off' effect – improving students' overall ability to express their thoughts precisely. Students need to use linkers in everyday conversation (and some 'conversational' linkers are practised in this book). However, it is in writing that linkers take on their most useful function.

Traditional grammar deals with some linkers under the heading of 'conjunctions': 'co-ordinating' conjunctions, such as *and*, *but*, and 'subordinating' conjunctions, such as *although, because*. However, in this book, both types of conjunction will be labelled as WITHIN-SENTENCE LINKERS, since their function is to join clauses within a single sentence.

Other linkers may be labelled in traditional grammar as 'sentence adverbs' or 'logical connecters'. They include items such as *however, in fact* and *in addition* which link ideas across two separate sentences, one sentence following another. In this book they are referred to as ACROSS-SENTENCE LINKERS.

Finally there are words and expressions which are labelled traditionally as prepositions, or prepositional phrases. These include expressions like *despite, owing to, during* and *as well as*. They mainly occur before noun phrases and *-ing* forms. In this book they are referred to as PHRASE LINKERS.

In this workbook, where the focus is on individual linkers, practice is mainly on single sentences or sentence pairs. However, longer contexts are provided when it is realistic to do so, especially when a variety of forms are practised. The material is designed to be suitable for students working on their own or for classroom use. Sometimes it would be misleading to say that one linker is definitely 'right' and another 'wrong' (though the answer key gives suggested answers): in such cases – as in **all** work on linkers – discussion should be encouraged.

The workbook is intended for adults and young adults who have to express themselves in study and work situations, and is appropriate for all students who have to present their ideas in an ordered way. The level is from lower-intermediate upwards, concentrating on intermediate. The book includes a review of linkers the student should already know and gives a thorough explanation of the types of linkers to be studied. It can be used on its own, or as supplementary material, e.g. within courses focusing on study skills or presentation skills. It is hoped that the content of the workbook will be found enjoyable as well as useful. The author and publishers welcome comments from users.

A first look at linkers, and some grammar

1 Within-sentence linkers

You already know words like *and*, *but*, *because*, *although*.

Susan sang two songs	*and*	Diana played the piano.
Susan sang two songs	*but*	she couldn't sing any more.
Susan sang two songs	*because*	everyone liked her singing.
Susan sang two songs	*although*	she had a sore throat.

We can call words like these 'linkers'. They are used to link ideas together.

In each sentence above there are two ideas, with a linker to join them. The ideas come in CLAUSES. A clause must have a VERB (usually a word to express an action) and a SUBJECT (usually a person or thing that controls the action). Notice that the sentences above have two clauses, but that a sentence can have **any** number of clauses.

In the examples above, the linker joins the clauses together **within one sentence**. In this book we will call words like *and*, *but*, *because*, *although* WITHIN-SENTENCE LINKERS.

2 Across-sentence linkers

There are other words which are used to join ideas together. For example:

Susan felt ill.	*However,*	she sang two songs.

Here, the sentences stay separate. *However* comes in the second sentence but there is a 'meaning' link across to the first sentence.

In this book we will call linkers like *however* ACROSS-SENTENCE LINKERS.

3 Phrase linkers

We can see a third type of linker in this example:

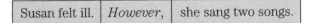

Susan sang two songs	*despite*	her sore throat.

Despite introduces the phrase 'her sore throat', which is a NOUN PHRASE. In this book we will call words like *despite* PHRASE LINKERS.

4 Picking out linkers

Read the sentences below. Underline the linkers.

1
I will keep on lovin' you, although you're far away…

5
Children under 12 are not admitted unless they are accompanied by an adult

2
Business has been poor this year. However, we expect an improvement in the year ahead.

6
Did you hear some strange noises during the night?

3
Can you teach my class this afternoon? The thing is, I'm taking my driving test…

7
Several matches have had to be cancelled today because of the weather.

4
Recent trials have shown that the drug is effective. It is also cheap to manufacture.

(a) Write down the within-sentence linkers.

_____

(b) Write down the across-sentence linkers.

_____

(c) Write down the phrase linkers.

_____

1 Addition, contrast, alternatives: *And, but, or*

All the linkers in this section, units 1–6, are within-sentence linkers.

1 Look at how we can join ideas together.

> GEORGE SAT DOWN   LUCY SAT BESIDE HIM (two main ideas, two main clauses) →
> George sat down *and* Lucy sat beside him. (ADDITION)
>
> I TRIED TO LIFT THE BOX   IT WAS TOO HEAVY (two main ideas, two main clauses) →
> I tried to lift the box *but* it was too heavy. (CONTRAST)
>
> WE CAN MEET TODAY   WE CAN MEET TOMORROW (two main ideas, two main clauses) →
> We can meet today *or* we can meet tomorrow. (ALTERNATIVES)

> **Notes**
> 1 *And* expresses ADDITION. One idea is added to another. *And* links two 'main ideas' expressed in two 'main clauses'.
> 2 *But* also brings equally important ideas together. The second idea CONTRASTS with the first: something happens differently from what you expect or hope.
> 3 *Or* also brings equally important ideas together, but the ideas are ALTERNATIVES. There is a choice between the second idea and the first.

Here are some well-known sayings in English. Complete them with *and*, *but* or *or*.

1

You can take a horse to water, _____ you can't make him drink.

2

Sink _____ swim.

3

You scratch my back _____ I'll scratch yours.

4

To be _____ not to be . . .

2 *And* in sentences with a series of same-subject verbs

> Tom got up *and* had breakfast. (2 verbs, each with the same subject. *And* before the second verb. We usually omit the subject before the second verb.)
>
> Tom got up, had breakfast *and* went to work. (3 verbs. *And* before the last verb, a comma before the second verb.)
>
> Tom got up, had breakfast, went to work *and* checked his mail. (4 verbs. *And* before the last verb, a comma before the second and third verbs.)

Underline verbs with the same subject in the sentences below.
Rewrite the sentences **if possible**, omitting subjects, and linking clauses with *and*.

1 An earthquake <u>struck</u> South America yesterday. It <u>caused</u> some damage. The damage occurred in a thinly-populated area.

   <u>An earthquake struck South America yesterday and caused some</u>
   <u>damage.</u>

2 The twentieth century has seen the development of antibiotics. Penicillin was developed in the 1940s. It has saved thousands of lives.

   _____

3 Rain will spread into all areas. Snow may fall on high ground. Drier weather is expected tomorrow.

   _____

4 The manager invited workers' representatives to the meeting. He explained the position to them. They had a long talk with him.

   _____

5 Susan and I went on a trip to Romania. We saw a lot of interesting sights. I spent two days in Italy on the way home.

   _____

6 Some delegates arrived by train. Others came by car. A few arrived by taxi.

   _____

7 A new nature reserve has been created in North Luanza. This is a unique area for wildlife. It has to be protected.

   _____

2 Contrast: *But, although, whereas*

1 *But* versus *although*

> I did not meet the Director, *but* I talked to the Sales Manager.
> (The speaker gives the same emphasis to 'meeting the Director' and 'talking to the Sales Manager'. Both ideas come in MAIN clauses.)
>
> *Although* I did not meet the Director, I talked to the Sales Manager.
> (The speaker gives more emphasis to the second part of the sentence, and less to 'meeting the Director' – perhaps because he has already mentioned it. He uses *although* before a SUBORDINATE clause.)
>
> **Note**
> *Although* comes before a subordinate clause. It often sounds more FORMAL than a sentence with *but*. It has the effect of binding the parts of the sentence more closely together, and putting more emphasis on the main clause.

Look at the notes below. Make sentences with a similar meaning using
(a) *but* (b) *although*.
Change the order if necessary.

1 Sally isn't very tall / Sally is good at basketball
    (a) <u>Sally isn't very tall, but she is good at basketball.</u>
    (b) <u>Although Sally isn't very tall, she is good at basketball.</u>

2 Mongolia does not have a large population / Mongolia is a large country
    (a) _____
    (b) _____

3 Jane likes to sing / Jane is not a very good singer
    (a) _____
    (b) _____

4 my car runs very well / I did not pay a lot of money for my car
    (a) _____
    (b) _____

5 Symtex is a smaller company than Tenbol / Symtex is more profitable than Tenbol
    (a) _____
    (b) _____

6 Van Gogh's paintings are now worth millions / Van Gogh did not sell any paintings during his lifetime

(a) _____

(b) _____

7 we did not play well / we won the match

(a) _____

(b) _____

8 a lot of novels are published every year / very few novels become bestsellers

(a) _____

(b) _____

9 there remain diseases for which there is no cure / smallpox has been eradicated

(a) _____

(b) _____

2 | *Whereas* (versus *although*)

Whereas Tom is interested in science, his twin brother Andrew is keen on art.

Although Tom likes science, his exam marks are poor.

Their house is on top of a hill, *whereas* ours is in the valley.

Notes
1 *Whereas* introduces a contrast between two people or things which are **in other ways similar**.
2 The clause with *whereas* can come first **or** later in the sentence.
3 *Although* does **not** suggest a similarity between two people/things.

Join the ideas using *whereas* or *although*.

1 Soccer is played with a round ball		a cats are solitary by nature.
2 Whales and dolphins are not fish		b rugby is played with an oval ball.
3 Mercury is a metal		c in Australia it starts in September.
4 English is a Germanic language	whereas	d they spend their lives in water.
5 Many people believe in astrology		e future vehicles may use hydrogen.
6 Dogs are pack animals		f people know it is harmful.
7 In Britain, spring starts in April	although	g it is a liquid at room temperature.
8 Present-day cars run on petrol		h French is descended from Latin.
9 Smoking is still a common habit		i it lacks any scientific proof.

1 whereas b _____   4 _____   7 _____

2 _____   5 _____   8 _____

3 _____   6 _____   9 _____

3 Reason and purpose: *Because, since, as, so that*

1 Expressing reasons with *because, since, as*

Because I lived further from the school than any other pupil, I was often the last to arrive. (*Because* brings out the IMPORTANCE of the reason. We could also use *as* or *since*, but they give less emphasis.)

He is only helping me *because* he knows my father. (Here the reason is the MAIN POINT of the sentence; *since* or *as* would be impossible.)

Since/As you've already met each other, I don't need to introduce you. (Here the reason is OBVIOUS to the listeners. *Because* would give the reason too much emphasis.)

Notes
1 *Because* EMPHASISES the reason. *As* and *since* suggest that the reason is OBVIOUS, or can be taken for granted.
2 *Since* can sound a little more formal than *as*, but the difference between *as* and *since* is more one of personal style. Do not use *as* if there is any confusion with *as* meaning 'while' (see Unit 5).

Underline the best answers. Sometimes both forms are possible.

1 Some people believe that Mozart died *because*/*since* he was poisoned.

2 John, *as/because* you speak French, I wondered if I could ask you some words?

3 We have a surprise for you. *Because/As* you have helped us so often, and for so many years, we would like to give you a present.

4 *Since/As* everyone is here, we can begin the meeting.

5 *Because/Since* we were young and inexperienced, we made a lot of mistakes.

6 Please allow Johnnie to leave school 15 minutes early, *as/because* he has a dentist's appointment.

7 I'll tell you why she lost her job! She was dismissed *since/because* she was lazy and inefficient!

8 'Why do you love me?' 'I love you *as/because* you understand me.'

9 I failed in the exam precisely *as/because* I didn't have time to study.

10 I ask the question 'Who will pay?' merely *as/because* we have received no financial details at all.

11 Following our letter of 16th April, *since/because* we have not heard from you, we assume that you have no objections to the proposal that was made to you.

2 **Expressing purpose with *so that*; contrast with *because***

> My daughter has taken a job after school *so that* she can buy a computer. (The *so that* clause expresses the PURPOSE in the girl's mind.)
> **Compare:**
> My daughter has taken a job *because* she has no money. (Lack of money is the REASON for taking a job.)
>
> **Note**
> The *so that* clause often contains *can, could, might, would* or *will* (modal verbs). It comes after the main clause.

Complete the sentences using (a) *so that*, (b) *because*. Write the sentences underneath.

1 Dave is driving fast		a the mosquitoes can't come in.
		b he can play games on it.
2 Louise wore a pink dress		c he's late.
		d he needs it for his work.
3 Ben has put nets on the window	so that	e Ann would recognise her at the airport.
	because	f he'll arrive on time.
4 Antoine has bought a computer		g she can get enough vitamins.
		h there are so many insects.
5 Nora eats green vegetables		i it was her favourite colour.
		j they're good for her health.

1 (a) _Dave is driving fast so that he'll arrive on time._

   (b) _____

2 (a) _____

   (b) _____

3 (a) _____

   (b) _____

4 (a) _____

   (b) _____

5 (a) _____

   (b) _____

4 Result: *So* (versus *so that*, *because*, etc.)

1 Introducing a result with *so*

I was hungry *so* I ate a sandwich. (*So* after a REASON, before a RESULT.)
Compare:
I ate a sandwich *because* I felt hungry. (*Because* before a reason.)
Since/As I felt hungry I ate a sandwich. (*Since/as* before a reason.)

Notes
1 *So* can have a comma before it: I was hungry, *so* I ate a sandwich.
2 We can change sentences with *so* into sentences with *because/since/as*, and vice versa.

Change the sentences below to sentences using the word given in brackets.
Change the order if necessary.

1   We had finished our work so we went home.
    <u>As we had finished our work we went home.</u>   (as)

2   Lise and Colin are having a party because they've got engaged.

    _____   (so)

3   Since this is the tourist season, accommodation may be expensive.

    _____   (so)

4   She wanted to read Dante in the original language, so she learnt Italian.

    _____   (because)

5   I'm not going to the disco because I don't like disco music.

    _____   (so)

6   You know what is in the letter, so I won't read it to you.

    _____   (since)

7   I wasn't present when the accident happened, so you can't blame me.

    _____   (as)

8   Meg is really angry because she wasn't invited to the wedding.

    _____   (so)

9   Jim had won £50 in a lottery, so he bought drinks for everybody.

    _____   (because)

10 We're here, so let's enjoy ourselves.

    _____   (since)

2 So versus so that

> There had been robberies in the neighbourhood, *so* everyone locked their doors. (*So* before the RESULT of the robberies. Comma before *so*.)
>
> I locked the door *so that* nobody could come in. (*So that* before the PURPOSE of locking the door.)
>
> **Note**
> People sometimes use *so* to mean *so that* in informal (spoken) English, but you should avoid this in written English.

Complete the sentences with *so* before a result, *so that* before a purpose.

1 The company is giving a prize

   (a) _so that_ it can get good publicity.

   (b) _____ we should try to win it.

2 Harold has gone to Italy

   (a) _____ he can't deal with your inquiry.

   (b) _____ he can meet some industrialists.

3 Tim bought a large house

   (a) _____ his parents could come and live with him.

   (b) _____ he had no money to spend on a car.

4 Mary got a bicycle

   (a) _____ she doesn't need to use her car so much now.

   (b) _____ she wouldn't have to use her car so much.

3 Mixed reason, result and purpose forms, units 3 and 4

Complete the newspaper report and letter below.

A *(report in the Pudston Gazette)*

Residents of Pudston are angry [1]_because_ the local council are planning to close Pudston Library. The decision to close has been taken [2]_____ financial savings can be made. '[3]_____ Pudston Library is the least used of all the libraries in the region, this was the obvious target,' said Council Chairman Bloggs. But Pudston people say this is unfair, [4]_____ the lack of use is due to limited opening hours. 'It's true that we don't use the library much,' said one, 'but that's just [5]_____ it's never open at times people can go there. It's only open on Thursday mornings for two hours, [6]_____ how can people use it?'

B *(letter to the editor of the Pudston Gazette)*

Dear Sir
It is time for Pudstonians to unite [7]_____ our voices may be heard. [8]_____ everyone in Pudston knows the importance of the library service, I urge all readers to protest to Chairman Bloggs. Our library is in danger just [9]_____ we have kept silent for too long. Now is the time to act. Mr Bloggs is due to visit Pudston next week [10]_____ he is giving a speech at Pudston School, [11]_____ let us all gather outside and tell him what we think of his plans.

⑤ Time: *While, as, until, before*

Time clauses can come at the beginning of the sentence **or** after the main clause. When the time clause comes first it usually has a comma after it.

1 *While* versus *as*

> *While* I was driving the car, you were asleep in the back. (*While* gives the idea that driving the car went on for a long time.)
>
> They arrived *while* we were having dinner. (*While* emphasises 'dinner' as a period of time.)
>
> They arrived *as* we were finishing our meal. (Finishing a meal doesn't take much time, so we can use *as* instead of *while*.)
>
> *As* I entered I heard a noise. ('Entered' is just a single action, not taking time, so we use *as* + simple past.)
>
> **Notes**
> 1 *As* and *while* can be used when one event happens at the same time as another.
> 2 *While* emphasises DURATION; it is more common with the continuous form of the verb. *As* does **not** emphasise duration; it is common with both the continuous and simple forms of the verb.

Here are some sentences from a crime novel. Complete them with *as* or *while* and a suitable form of the verb in brackets. More than one answer may be possible.

1 _____As_____ Sam __opened__ (open)

the door he heard a shot ring out.

2 _____ the police _____

(investigate) the crime they received letters

making accusations.

3 'You'll have time to be sorry for your crime

_____ you _____ (rot) in

prison!' shouted Gladys.

4 _____ Harry _____ (sail) his

yacht round the world, his wife was

planning to kill him.

5 The details became clearer _____

detectives _____ (begin) to

examine the scene of the crime.

6 _____ the light of his torch

_____ (move) round the room, a

terrible sight met his eyes.

7 'Look behind you _____ you

_____ (drive) to see if anyone is

following you,' warned the detective.

8 All these events took place _____ the

couple _____ (stay) at their

London home.

14

2 *Before* versus *until*; mixed time forms

> *Before* Columbus sailed to America, he obtained money from the Queen of Spain. (Two separate events: 1 'obtaining money', 2 'sailing to America'.)
>
> Columbus sailed west *until* he reached America. (Reaching America marked the END of Columbus's voyage west.)
>
> **Note**
> *Before* simply shows that one event comes before another, SEPARATE event.
> *Until* is used when Event 2 is 'joined' to Event 1, and marks the END of Event 1.

(Mixed forms) Complete the sentences below with *as*, *while*, *before* or *until*.
Note: We use *while*, not *as* when the verb 'to be' is the main verb in the clause.
For example:
While you *are* here you can do some work.

1 Suddenly, ___ as ___ we were getting into the bus, the rain came on.

2 Don't wait up for me – it'll be midnight _____ I get back.

3 I won't be satisfied _____ I've worked out the answer to this puzzle!

4 _____ the teacher was out of the class, some pupils wrote a message on the board.

5 We cannot buy any more equipment this year _____ new funds arrive.

6 There's time to ge a sandwich from the cafeteria _____ the next class begins.

7 You can talk to the guests _____ I'm doing the cooking.

8 _____ the clock struck midnight, everybody wished each other a Happy New Year.

9 (*what Carlos wrote on his Valentine card to his girlfriend, who lives abroad*)

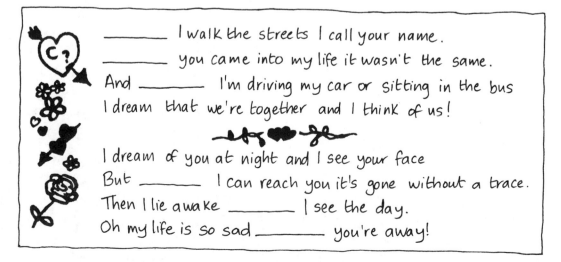

_____ I walk the streets I call your name.
_____ you came into my life it wasn't the same.
And _____ I'm driving my car or sitting in the bus
I dream that we're together and I think of us!

I dream of you at night and I see your face
But _____ I can reach you it's gone without a trace.
Then I lie awake _____ I see the day.
Oh my life is so sad _____ you're away!

6 Condition: *If, provided (that), in case, if not, unless*

1 *If* versus *provided* and *in case*

I'll go to college *if/provided* I pass the exam. (Both *if* and *provided* are possible. *Provided* is stronger. It suggests a condition standing in the way of something you WANT to happen.)

I'll accept the job *provided* I'm allowed to do things my own way. (We use *provided* for conditions that someone LAYS DOWN before agreeing to something.)

If the earth gets warmer, sea levels will rise. (We cannot use *provided* here – we are not talking about things that people WANT to happen.)

I'll take a sleeping bag *in case* I have to stay overnight. (*In case* means 'as a PRECAUTION against some possible trouble or danger'.)

Note
Provided can also occur as *provided that*. Both forms are common.

Complete the sentences below with *if, provided,* or *in case*.

1 Linda agreed to lend us her car,
   <u>provided</u> we paid her for the petrol.

2 We must take first-aid equipment with us
   _____ any member of the group
   gets injured.

3 I am totally against the plan to widen the
   road! _____ the road is widened,
   cars will simply go faster – there will be no
   improvement in safety!

4 Farmers expect to have good crops
   _____ there is rain during the
   next month.

5 _____ the teacher finds out what
   you've done he'll be really angry.

6 Listen! I want to make the matter absolutely
   clear to you, _____ there's any
   misunderstanding. I can't stand Bill and I
   won't work with him!

7 I advise you to carry your passport with you
   at all times _____ you need to
   give proof of your identity.

8 You have nothing to fear from the police
   _____ you tell the truth.

9 'Will you take on the job of secretary?' 'Yes,
   on one condition – I'll do it, _____
   someone helps me with typing out letters.'

10 The walkers decided to take warm clothing
    _____ the weather worsened.

> We can use **both** *if not* **and** *unless* in these sentences:
> He'll die *if* he doesn't receive / *unless* he receives medical treatment.
> (= Medical treatment will STOP him from dying.)
>
> *If* I don't hear from you / *Unless* I hear from you I'll continue as planned.
> (= Hearing from you will STOP me from continuing.)
>
> We **must** use *if not* (**not** *unless*) in these sentences:
> I'll be sad *if* you don't invite me to your party. (= NOT inviting me will
> START sadness in me.)
>
> He'd get good exam results *if* he didn't play computer games all the time.
> (= NOT playing computer games would START good exam results.)
>
> **Notes**
> *Unless* **or** *if not* can be used when doing something will END a situation.
> *If not* must be used when **not** doing something will BEGIN a new situation.

Here are some sentences that were spoken
at a party. Choose the best way of completing
each sentence. Sometimes both (a) and
(b) are possible.

1 I'm sure Jim is going to have a nervous
   breakdown (a) *if he doesn't learn to
   relax* (b) *unless he learns to relax.*   Both

2 She'd look lovely (a) *unless she wore*
   (b) *if she didn't wear* such
   old-fashioned clothes.   _____

3 I'll be your friend for life (a) *if you don't tell Gisela* (b) *unless
   you tell Gisela* that you saw me with Annabel last night.   _____

4 I've told Joe to keep away from my girlfriend. (a) *If he doesn't,*
   (b) *Unless he does,* I'll punch his face in!   _____

5 Their lawyer says that they intend to take me to court
   (a) *unless I pay* (b) *if I don't pay* the bill immediately.   _____

6 'Should I accept his offer?' 'Definitely! You'd be throwing away a
   great opportunity (a) *if you didn't accept it* (b) *unless you
   accepted it.*'   _____

7 It'll be your own fault (a) *if you don't win* (b) *unless you win* the
   contract to build the new hospital.   _____

8 Why did you tell Marie about me and Bill? (a) *If she doesn't
   want to speak to me again* (b) *Unless she wants to speak to me
   again* I'll blame you.   _____

7 Addition: *Also, moreover, in addition, besides*

1 *Also*: Position in the sentence

> They asked for food. *They also wanted* money. (*Also* between the SUBJECT and the VERB.)
>
> She is extremely clever. She **is** *also* very efficient. (*Also* after *is, are, was, were*.)
>
> In my speech, I'll be looking at the present situation. I *shall also* be making predictions for the future. (*Also* after auxiliary verb *shall*.)
>
> **Note**
> *Also* is common in speech and writing. We usually put it:
> a) between the subject of the sentence and a 'simple' verb
> b) after *is, are, was, were*
> c) after auxiliary verbs such as *will, can*, etc.

Insert *also* in the sentences below. Draw a line (/) to show where it should go and write *also* above the line.

1 You can buy computers in shops. You can / get them by mail order.
                                                    also

2 Dr Cox was a keen tennis player. He had been a fine athlete in his youth.

3 Fire alarms must be tested every month. Emergency lighting should be checked regularly.

4 Harry has several dogs and cats. He has a number of more exotic creatures.

5 Liz is organising the competition. She is going to present the prizes.

6 Signor Ginelli owns a shipping business. He runs an oil company.

7 The view from the balcony was marvellous. The closeness of the house to the city suited them.

2 *Moreover, in addition, besides*

> The rent for the building was reasonable. *Moreover*, the location was perfect. (*Moreover* when two equally important facts are given; rather formal.)
>
> The company was reorganised. New members of staff were recruited. *In addition*, the managers were given new responsibilities. (*In addition* often comes in a list of ACTIONS; rather formal or factual in tone.)
>
> I don't want the job. It would mean too much travelling. *Besides*, the salary is too low. (*Besides* is often used when we list different reasons; more common in speech than in writing.)
>
> **Note**
> *Moreover, in addition* and *besides* usually have a comma after them and can begin a sentence.

(Mixed 'addition' forms) Complete the newspaper reports below with *moreover*, *in addition*, *also* or *besides*.

A Thieves raided an art gallery in Newgate last night and made off with several items of jewellery. ¹ <u>In addition</u>, a substantial sum of money was stolen. Inspector Barlow of Newgate CID said that there had been a number of similar thefts from private houses recently, and there had ² _____ been several break-ins at office premises.

Councillor Dodds said that cuts in policing were partly responsible for the increase in crime.³ _____ , unemployment had risen in the Newgate area, and he believed this was an important factor. 'Crime is increasing along with worsening social conditions,' he said. '⁴ _____ , there simply aren't enough police officers on our streets nowadays.'

B

Singer Ricki Moor has had to cancel his tour of Britain in June. He has ⁵ _____ decided not to give any further live performances until the autumn. 'The financial arrangements were unsatisfactory,' he said. '⁶ _____ , we need time to prepare our new album.' Moor has contracted soul-singer Nina Hooper to sing with him on the album. ⁷ _____ , he has hired producer John Standish, regarded as one of the best professionals in the music business. Moor's career has had its ups and downs in recent years, and his last album had only modest success. ⁸ _____ , there were widespread reports of difficulties in his marriage to actress Jan Lecompte. Whatever the truth in this, it seems that he is putting the problems behind him and starting a new chapter in his life.

8 Contrast: *However, nevertheless*

1 *However*: Use and position in the sentence

> Beethoven became deaf at the age of 32. *However*, he still managed to compose great music. (Two contrasting facts about the same person.)
>
> Haydn wrote 104 symphonies. *However*, his pupil Beethoven wrote only nine. (Contrasting facts about two different people.)
>
> Ann wanted to continue the discussion. The others, *however*, wanted to finish the meeting. (*However* later in the sentence.)

> **Note**
> *However* is rather formal. It usually begins a sentence and has a comma after it, but can also come later. You may find it (a) before the main verb, (b) after adverbs like *sometimes*, *often*, *usually*, *generally*, etc.

Look at the notes below. At (a) rewrite the notes using *however* at the beginning of a sentence. At (b) show an **alternative** position for *however*. You may need to change the order of the notes.

1 the Ancient Greeks discovered steam power / they did not use it industrially

    (a) The Ancient Greeks discovered steam power. However, they did not use it industrially.

    (b) _____

2 my sister eats meat / my brother is a strict vegetarian

    (a) _____

    (b) _____

3 modern computers occupy much less space / early computers took up whole rooms

    (a) _____

    (b) _____

4 occasionally snakebites cause death / most snakebites are non-fatal

    (a) _____

    (b) _____

5 some babies walk at nine months / in general babies walk around thirteen months

    (a) _____

    (b) _____

Which sentences give contrasting facts about the **same** people/things? _____

Which sentences deal with contrasts between **different** people/things? _____

2 *However* versus *nevertheless*

> 'Linkers' are important. *However,/Nevertheless,* they are not always taught. (Two contrasting facts about the SAME thing. We can use *however* **or** *nevertheless*. *Nevertheless* is stronger, suggesting OPPOSING facts.)
>
> The French exam was easy. *However,* the chemistry exam was difficult. (Contrast between two DIFFERENT things. Here we **cannot** use *nevertheless*, as there is no real opposition between the facts. The two exams are 'independent'.)
>
> We worked hard, *but nevertheless* we were unable to finish the job in time. (*Nevertheless* after *but*: we **cannot** use *however* after *but*.)

Captain Crock is reporting on a planet he is exploring. Underline the correct form. Sometimes **both** forms are possible.

1 The creatures on this planet appear to be intelligent.

 However,/Nevertheless, they have not tried to make contact with us.

2 The area to the north is desert. *However,/Nevertheless,*

 the area to the south has thick forests.

3 Several of our crew have had a strange illness, but *nevertheless,/*

 however, we intend to continue with our exploration.

4 The planet has two suns. One of them is like our own sun.

 Nevertheless,/However, the other is blue in colour.

5 The planet is beautiful, but *however,/nevertheless,*

 there is something frightening about it.

6 I have ordered Mercury Brigade to explore to the south.

 However,/Nevertheless, Mars Brigade will stay to guard the spaceship.

7 I was bitten by a giant ant this morning. *However,/Nevertheless,*

 I shall continue . . .

 (Here Captain Crock's report ends.)

9 Contrast and comparison: *On the other hand, by contrast, on the contrary, conversely*

The linkers in this unit often occur within a larger, comparative 'picture'.
They can all begin a sentence, and usually have a comma after them.

1 *On the other hand* versus *by contrast*

To strangers he appeared sarcastic and ill-tempered. *On the other hand*, his friends found him kind-hearted and generous. (Contrasting sides of the SAME person are brought together.)

John Sykes was a mean, ill-tempered man. *By contrast*, his brother was kind-hearted and generous. (Two DIFFERENT people are contrasted.)

Notes
1 *On the other hand* introduces a contrast which is part of a SINGLE OVERALL PICTURE; often the contrast is between different 'sides' of the same person or thing; it is common both in speech and writing.
2 *By contrast* (also *in contrast*) introduces a clear contrast between two different people or things; it is rather formal.

The sentences below can be completed with both (a) and (b).
Insert *On the other hand* or *By contrast*.

1 Schools nowadays do not encourage memorisation.

   (a) <u>On the other hand</u> , pupils do more projects

      and investigative work than before.

   (b) _____ , pupils in former times

      had to learn many things by heart.

2 Lang (1973) reported good results using the drug Trisulphin.

   (a) _____ , he also listed a number of unpleasant side-effects.

   (b) _____ , a newer drug, Enzofalm, appeared to have little effect.

3 Tennis players often behave badly without losing points.

   (a) _____ , football players are

      immediately sent off the field.

   (b) _____ , they are sometimes

      fined for bad behaviour.

4 The original Salko GL was not an advanced car, technically.

   (a) _____ , the new model is a remarkable technical achievement.

   (b) _____ , it was inexpensive, comfortable, and easy to maintain.

5 In old age, people may lose some of their mental agility.

   (a) _____ , they often gain a greater

   understanding of life.

   (b) _____ , young people are often

   very quick in absorbing information.

6 Working from home is comfortable and convenient.

   (a) _____ , one may miss the chance to discuss things with colleagues.

   (b) _____ , travelling every day to an office is tiring and expensive.

2 *On the contrary* versus *conversely*

> The economy will not improve this year. *On the contrary*, it is likely to get
> worse. (The second sentence strongly REJECTS the idea of an improvement. It
> STRENGTHENS THE NEGATIVE of 'will not improve'.)
>
> In the northern hemisphere, the summer months are from July to September.
> *Conversely*, in the southern hemisphere, the summer is from January to March.
> (The SAME facts from the OPPOSITE POINT OF VIEW.)

Insert *on the contrary* and *conversely* in the sentences below.
Draw a line (/) to show where the words should go. Alter punctuation as necessary. Write the
changes above the sentences.

1 Over 90% of the top group of students passed the exam. /Only 10% of the lowest
    Conversely, only

   group achieved the required standard.

2 I do not blame the author for punching the reviewer on the nose. I think he was

   completely justified in doing so.

3 I have never heard John say anything bad about you. He's always spoken well of you.

4 The proportion of people renting houses has declined over the years. The

   percentage of people buying their own home has increased.

5 If a triangle has two equal sides, it must have two equal angles. If there are two

   equal angles, it must have two equal sides.

6 Our firm has no objections to employing older people. Applications from people

   over 50 will be welcomed.

10 Results and conclusions: *Thus, therefore*

1 *Thus*: Meanings and patterns

> Modern societies need educated workers. *Thus*, we must increase spending on education. (*Thus* = 'so', 'for this reason'. The first sentence explains the second sentence.)
>
> My talk will be in two parts. *Thus*, I shall begin with the historical background and then deal with current ideas. (*Thus* = 'the details are as follows'; the second sentence gives details to explain the first.)
>
> We shall spend more money on education and *thus* give our young people hope for the future. (*Thus* = 'by doing this'.)

> **Notes**
> 1 *Thus* (with a comma after it) is a useful general-purpose linker when one sentence EXPLAINS another. It is used mainly in formal writing and speech.
> 2 *Thus* (often *and thus*) can also mean 'by this method', 'by doing this'. Notice that there is no comma after it.

(*Political reports*) Insert *thus* or *and thus* in the sentences below.
Make two sentences whenever you can. Alter punctuation as necessary.

1 The president was very unpopular his resignation did not come as a surprise.

   <u>The president was very unpopular. Thus, his resignation did not come as a</u>
   <u>surprise.</u>

2 The government intends to reduce taxes increase its popularity.

3 There had been riots in the streets the army decided to take control.

4 The police fired tear gas managed to disperse the protesters.

5 The government has announced a programme of reform it will improve social benefits for the poor.

6 The health minister claimed that great progress had been made 240 new hospitals had been built.

7 The opposition parties voted against the proposal prevented it from becoming law.

_____

8 The new minister, Mrs Duras, is energetic she will probably adopt new policies.

_____

2 *Therefore* **and** *thus*

> The economic situation was poor. We *therefore* postponed our plans for expansion.
> (*Therefore* before the main verb; **compare** *Thus, we postponed . . .*)
>
> The economic situation was poor. We were *therefore* unable to proceed with our plans.
> (*Therefore* after the verb 'to be'; **compare** *Thus, we were unable . . .*)
>
> **Note**
> *Therefore* (without a comma) can be used instead of *thus* to state a result.
> Usually it does **not** begin a sentence. It goes (a) after the subject of the sentence, before
> the main verb, (b) after the verb 'to be', or any modal auxiliary verb (*is, are, was, were,*
> *will, should, may, can, could, might, must*).

(*Sentences from official letters*)
Rewrite the sentences below as
two sentences, using *therefore*
in a suitable place. Alter the
punctuation as necessary.

1 Our department does not deal with these matters. Thus, we are unable to help.
   <u>Our department does not deal with these matters. We are therefore</u>
   <u>unable to help.</u>

2 As the books you borrowed are overdue, you should return them immediately.

_____

3 I wish to cancel my insurance policy as I no longer have a car.

_____

4 We have received many complaints, so we must ask you to reduce the noise level.

_____

5 You are a valued customer. Thus, I am sending you our new catalogue.

_____

6 Because you sent the money on 16th June, payment arrived several days late.

_____

11 Results and conclusions: *Hence, consequently*; mixed reason/result forms

1 Hence and consequently

> One side of the rectangle is 4 cm and the other is 3 cm. *Hence*, the total area is 12 cm². (*Hence* = 'it follows logically that'.)
>
> The town was built on the River Cam: *hence* the name Cambridge. (*Hence* = 'that is the reason for'; there is no verb in the phrase after *hence*.)
>
> The bank refused to help the company. *Consequently*, it went bankrupt. (*Consequently* = 'as a direct result'.)
>
> **Notes**
> 1 *Hence* is like *thus* but even more formal; used mainly for conclusions that a person could arrive at using LOGIC or REASONING.
> 2 When *hence* means 'that is the reason for', it has no verb after it. It usually comes after a colon (:), semi-colon (;), comma (,) or dash (–).
> 3 *Consequently* is also formal. It is used mainly to describe DIRECT RESULTS and tends to be used when describing actions/events at a particular time, place, etc.

Change these sentences with *so* into formal, two-sentence statements using *hence* or *consequently*. Alter punctuation as necessary.

1 There is no defect in the fuel system of the car, so the fault appears to lie with the electrical system. <u>There is no defect in the fuel system of the car. Hence, the fault appears to lie with the electrical system.</u>

2 Several teachers are ill, so the school will be closed until further notice. _____

3 The ship suffered damage in a storm, so it had to go into port for repairs. _____

4 There is no evidence of damage to the door, so the thieves must have entered the building through the window. _____

5 Over 90% of our patients improved after taking the drug, so the drug can be regarded as an effective treatment for the disease. _____

26

6 Calcium hydroxide is an alkali, so it reacts with acids to form a salt plus water. _____

_____

7 The temperature in Saudi Arabia can reach 50°C, so a lot of business is done early in the day.

_____

8 The soldiers in the Pacifican Army were poorly paid, so morale was extremely low.

_____

2 Mixed reason/result forms

Choose the best answer in the sentences below.

1 I'll be out all day *so/hence* I'll leave your lunch in the oven.

2 John copies the answers from his brother and *hence/thus* achieves good marks.

3 Poachers shoot elephants for their ivory. *Consequently/Because* the number of elephants is decreasing.

4 Mr Cox is ill and will *therefore/since* be unable to lecture today.

5 There is no record of the transaction on our files. *As/Thus*, there is no proof that the transaction ever took place.

6 Temperatures are likely to fall *as/consequently* cold weather is moving in from the north.

7 Lisa is getting married: *so/hence* the ring on her finger.

8 The costs of producing the magazine have risen steadily. We are *therefore/hence* raising the subscription to $20 for four issues.

9 Benjamin Roe has ambitions to become the world's leading newspaper proprietor: *hence/consequently* his purchase of the *New York Globe*.

10 We are planning a series of conferences next summer. *Thus/Therefore*, there will be a weekend devoted to 'Hospital Reform', a day on 'New Technology', and a week on 'Health in the twenty-first Century'.

11 *Since/Hence* the three sides of the triangle are equal in length, each of the angles must also be equal.

12 Alternatives: *Alternatively, otherwise, instead*

1 *Alternatively* versus *otherwise*

> You could take the exam in May. *Alternatively*, you could wait till August. (= There is a CHOICE. The person might want to do either.)
>
> You could take the first bus, *or alternatively* you could travel later in the day. (*Alternatively* after *or*.)
>
> You'd better go now. *Otherwise* you'll miss your train. (= There is no real choice. The person does not want to miss the train.)
>
> **Notes**
> 1 *Alternatively* is used when there is a REAL choice. It often goes with *can* or *could*. It can come after *or*.
> 2 *Otherwise* has the idea of 'if not'. It suggests a WARNING, not a real choice.

Put the notes below in order and make sentences using *otherwise* or *alternatively*. Sometimes you can make one **or** two sentences.

1 he may have an accident / I hope he drives carefully

   I hope he drives carefully. Otherwise he may have an accident.

2 if the goods are faulty we can replace them / we can give you a refund

3 you could get one tomorrow morning / there's a plane tonight

4 he'll fail / Tom will have to work harder

5 we must improve our profits / we could go bankrupt

6 you can pay for it in instalments / you can buy the car now

> We don't make any products by hand nowadays. *Instead*, we use computer-controlled robots. (*Instead* often comes after a negative sentence.)
>
> We don't make our products by hand. We use robots *instead*. (*Instead* at the end of a sentence – sounds less formal than at the beginning.)
>
> They advised us to fly, *but instead* we decided to come by train. (*Instead* after *but*.)
>
> We shall cease hand-production, *and instead* utilise industrial robots. (*Instead* after *and*.)
>
> **Note**
> *Instead* is used when one action 'takes the place' of another. It often comes after a negative sentence. It can begin a sentence (plus comma), or come after *but* or *and* (usually no comma). It can also come at the **end** of a sentence, but this sounds slightly less formal.

Insert *instead* in a suitable position in the sentences below. Draw a line (/) to show where it should go. Alter punctuation as necessary. Write the changes above the sentences.

instead
1 We gave up the idea of moving house and / decided to extend our existing house.

2 Cars will not run on petrol in future they will run on hydrogen.

3 They hoped to make money on the stock exchange but lost everything

4 We no longer post letters to Hong Kong we send faxes.

5 Typewriters are becoming obsolete most writing is done on word processors.

3 **Mixed forms**

Complete the texts below with *alternatively*, *otherwise* or *instead*.

A (*a government minister is speaking*)
We must reduce public spending.
¹   Otherwise   , we will never defeat inflation. We must stop spending money which we have not earned, and ²_____ look at every branch of government to see if savings are possible. Savings may be possible in the health budget. ³_____ , we may be able to cut spending on education.

B (*giving directions to a driver*)
I wouldn't take the A4 if I were you – the traffic on it is very heavy. ⁴_____ , I would take the B402 to Southam. But be careful to take the ring road round Southam. ⁵_____ , you'll get stuck in the town centre. Then take the B438 north, or ⁶_____ you could go onto the motorway.

13 Rephrasing and correcting: *In other words, or rather, at least*

> He did not reach the required standard. *In other words*, he failed. (The second sentence EXPLAINS the meaning of the first, using simpler language.)
>
> It was late at night when he came home. *Or rather*, it was early in the morning. (The second sentence CORRECTS the first by giving more exact information.)
>
> He's asleep. *At least*, his eyes are closed. ('Eyes closed' doesn't go so far as 'being asleep'.)
>
> He's leaving on Monday – *or at least*, he says he is. (*At least* after *or*.)
>
> **Notes**
> 1 We use *in other words* when we EXPLAIN a point, often in simpler language.
> 2 We use *or rather* to CORRECT something we have just said.
> 3 We use *at least* when we correct ourselves with a 'weaker' statement, one which doesn't go so far. It usually takes a comma. It can begin a sentence, or come after *or*.

1 Mr Perkins doesn't like Bert, his daughter's boyfriend. Complete what he says about Bert, using *in other words, or rather, at least*.

1 He wastes his money on useless things.

   <u>Or rather</u> , he wastes my daughter's money.

2 You can't trust him. _____ , you can

   trust him to tell lies.

3 He's 'allergic' to work. _____ , he's a lazy

   good-for-nothing.

4 He spends his whole life in the pub. _____ , he's there most nights of the week.

5 Last night he borrowed a friend's motor bike. _____ , he took it without permission.

6 The police followed him and found he was going at 125 kilometres an hour – or _____ , he was over the speed limit.

7 They also tested his eyesight and found that he was driving with 'defective vision'. _____ , he should have been wearing glasses.

8 I'll be surprised if he doesn't go to prison for it. _____ , he'll be banned from driving.

9 Of course he'll be very sorry now – or _____ he'll say he is.

10 It's time his association with my daughter ended. _____ , it's time she got rid of him.

14 'Main point' linkers: *Anyway, in any case, the thing is*

1 *Anyway*

Perhaps the interviewers liked the answers I gave, or perhaps they were impressed by my experience. *Anyway*, I got the job. (Getting the job is the main point – the reasons don't matter.)

The committee will discuss the matter shortly. *In any case*, you will be notified within the next two weeks. (*In any case* used in a formal letter.)

Maybe I'll phone you tomorrow. *In any case*, I'll let you know by the end of the week. (*In any case* in speech; we could also use *anyway* here.)

Notes
1 *Anyway* and *In any case* show that we are coming (or returning) to the MAIN POINT, and that what we have just said is not so important. The meaning is often 'whatever the truth may be'.
2 *Anyway* is used mainly in speech. *In any case* can be used both in speech and formal writing.
3 We sometimes use *anyhow* and *at any rate* in conversation with the same meaning as *anyway*.

In the passages below, underline the sentences which could begin with *anyway* or *in any case*.

1 I'm not going to the party, I don't like parties much. <u>I'm too tired</u>. I'll probably just stay at home and watch TV tonight.

2 We are confident that our equipment will provide years of useful service. We have thousands of satisfied customers all over the world. If a fault should develop, we guarantee that our engineers will carry out immediate repairs, free of charge.

3 Both Adams (1974) and Bentley (1991) found that language learning improved when the audio-tactile method was used. Gonzales (1985) also reported some success with this approach. It appears that the technique will play a part in language teaching in future. Nevertheless, further research is needed to determine how it can be used most effectively.

4 Eike phoned the office. She says she isn't feeling well. She thinks it might be flu. She won't be at work today.

5 We'd better go now. We've got a lot of work to do tomorrow. It's getting late. If we don't go now we'll miss the last bus.

In which passages would you use *in any case* (**not** *anyway*)? —————

> Our firm is doing badly. *The thing is*, there is no market for our goods. ('No market' is the explanation of why the firm is doing badly.)
>
> I'm worried about Cathy. *The thing is*, she hates her school. (The fact that Cathy hates her school explains why the speaker is worried.)
>
> JOHN: Why won't you marry me, Michaela?
> MICHAELA: *The thing is*, John, I don't want to marry anyone. (Michaela explains why she won't marry John.)

> **Note**
> *The thing is* comes before the main point, when the main point also acts as the EXPLANATION of a previous sentence. It is used mainly in conversation.

Choose between *anyway* and *the thing is* in the conversations below.

1  A Are you doing anything this weekend?
   B No, nothing special.
   A *Anyway*, / *The thing is*, I'm having some friends round for dinner. Would you like to come?

2 A Louise looks very happy today.
  B Haven't you heard? She and Harry are getting married.
  A That's nice. They've been friends for ages. Maybe she told Harry it was now or never.
  B Maybe so. *Anyway*, / *The thing is*, they've finally made the decision.

3 A Did Paolo get the job he applied for?
  B No. I thought he had a good chance of getting it. Maybe they thought he was too old.
    Anyway, / *The thing is*, he didn't get it.

4 A I hear Marie passed her biology exams.
  B She had no problems at all. *Anyway*, / *The thing is*, she has such a good memory, she just needs to look at a diagram once and she remembers it.

5 A What do you think of Joe Glenn's paintings?
  B Not much. *Anyway*, / *The thing is*, he has simply no idea about colour.

15 'Extra point' linkers: *By the way, incidentally;* mixed 'main' and 'extra' forms

1 *By the way, incidentally*

I met Dita in Athens. *By the way*, she sends you her regards. She says she's going to stay for another year. (*By the way* used to insert an extra point into the conversation. The extra point is not so important to the speaker.)

So that's the situation. *By the way*, this is a secret, so don't mention it to anyone. (Here the extra point about secrecy is **very** important.)

Our German subsidiary has sent an order for another 5,000 copies of the book. *Incidentally*, their sales are up 45% this year. (*Incidentally* before an additional fact. *By the way* is also possible, but sounds less 'factual'.)

Notes
1 *By the way* and *incidentally* can both occur in speech. *Incidentally* sounds a little more factual/formal, but the difference is more one of personal style. In writing, *incidentally* is more likely to occur.
2 *By the way* and *incidentally* can introduce an interesting (but not important) fact about a topic – as if you were saying something 'in brackets'. However, they can also introduce points that are VERY important to you.

Read the sentences below and decide on a suitable order (more than one may be possible). Before which sentence would you put the linker (*by the way* or *incidentally*)?

1 (a) Four of them were absent.
  (b) It seems George Michael is their favourite singer.
  (c) I did a survey of the students in the class today.

    Order ___c-a-b___ ; linker before ___(a) Incidentally___

2 (a) Have you seen her recently?
  (b) She says she's enjoying her holiday.
  (c) I got a postcard from Lisa MacDonald this morning.

    Order _____ ; linker before _____

3 (a) Twenty-eight new students enrolled today.
  (b) A lot of them seem to be from eastern Europe.
  (c) We'll divide them into two groups, OK?

    Order _____ ; linker before _____

4 (a) The opening ceremony is on TV.
  (b) The Olympic Games start tomorrow.
  (c) How many medals did we get last time?

    Order _____ ; linker before _____

5 (a) Do please clean everything up after you.
   (b) It's your turn for the sauna tonight.
   (c) It's reserved for you from eight till nine thirty.

   Order _____ ; linker before _____

2   Mixed 'main point' and 'extra point' forms, units 14 and 15

Insert a suitable linker in the passages and conversations below.

1 A   Are you coming to the lecture this evening?

   B   Yes, I expect so. ___By the way___ , how long is it supposed to last?

2 The report from the committee suggests that the tax on petrol should not be
   introduced. Such an increase would be harmful to industry. _____ ,
   it would be unfair to motorists living in rural areas.

3 The latest news is that Thomson has recovered from his injury and will play
   for Rovers tonight. _____ , new figures show that Thomson was
   the highest-paid player in the league last season.

4 Chris, you couldn't by any chance lend me £10 till tomorrow, could you?
   _____ , I forgot to go to the bank this morning.

5 A   Are you getting time off from work to play in the competition?

   B   I haven't asked for time off. My boss wouldn't be keen on the idea. _____ ,
       the competition doesn't start till 6 p.m., so there shouldn't be any problem.

6 It was a good result for Vampyra, the Transylvanian athlete, who
   won the silver medal in the 5,000 metres. _____ ,
   that was Transylvania's first medal in these games.

7 A   I hear that Charles and his wife are separating.

   B   Well, that shouldn't surprise anyone. _____ ,
       they haven't been getting on well for years.

8 A   So, are you off to do your shopping now?

   B   Yes, I've got a lot to do. _____ ,
       could you possibly give me a lift into town if you're
       going that way? I didn't bring my car this morning.

16 Reality: (but) in fact, (and) indeed

1 Two uses of in fact

> I don't like him. *In fact*, I can't stand him. (The second sentence STRENGTHENS the first.)
>
> People think I don't like Harry, *but in fact*, he's a good friend. (The second clause CONTRADICTS the idea in the previous clause.)

Put the notes below in order and make sentences, using *in fact* or *but in fact*.

1 it rained all day
the weatherman had promised sunny weather

The weatherman had promised sunny weather, but in fact, it rained all day.

2 Dynamo are the best team in the country
Dynamo are a very good team

_____

_____

3 research on anti-viral drugs is making good progress
a cure for many deadly diseases is only a few years away

_____

_____

4 we thought we might arrive even earlier.
we expected to reach our destination by midday

_____

5 the expedition hoped to climb the mountain by August
it was mid-September before they could begin the ascent

_____

_____

2 Two uses of *indeed*

> Our results this year have been satisfactory. *Indeed*, they are the best results we have had for several years. (A formal report; the second sentence STRENGTHENS the first. The meaning is the same as *in fact* but *indeed* is more formal.)
>
> He was said to be 110 years old, *and indeed*, he could remember events from long ago. Nevertheless, I never found out his real age. (= I ADMIT that he was old, but have DOUBTS about whether or not he was 110.)
>
> **Notes**
> 1 *Indeed* sounds a little more formal than *in fact*. We can use it instead of *in fact* when we want to STRENGTHEN our previous sentence. (Notice that we **cannot** use *indeed* when there is a 'contradicting' meaning.)
> 2 We can use *and indeed* when there is some evidence to support a fact, but we still have DOUBTS. The meaning is 'it is certainly true that . . .'.

Insert *indeed* in the sentences below **if possible**. Draw a line (/) to show where it should go. Alter punctuation as necessary. Write the changes above the sentences.

Indeed, he

1 Webb is a fine athlete. / He is the best athlete in these games.

2 The newspapers praised him highly, and he did an excellent job. However, other people deserved just as much credit.

3 Linda was blamed for the accident, but it wasn't her fault at all.

4 Hudson's book did not sell well at first. The publishers considered dropping it from their list. However, it is now a bestseller.

5 We shall have to work with each other even if we don't get on well.

3 (Mixed forms) Choose the best way of beginning the sentences below, (a) or (b).

1 (a) The disease is serious. In fact, . . .
   (b) The disease is serious, but in fact . . .
      . . . it is fatal in over 60% of cases.

2 (a) Muller has developed a vaccine for it, and indeed . . .
   (b) Muller has developed a vaccine for it. In fact . . .
      . . . his work gives some cause for hope. However, it appears that the vaccine is only partially effective.

3 (a) At first Muller claimed to have found a 'cure'. In fact . . .
   (b) At first Muller claimed to have found a 'cure', but in fact . . .
      . . . further research showed such claims were exaggerated.

4 (a) Cases of the disease will increase throughout the 1990s. Indeed . . .
   (b) Cases of the disease will increase throughout the 1990s, but in fact . . .
      . . . it may become a world health problem in the twenty-first century.

17 Reality: *Actually, as a matter of fact*; mixed 'reality' forms

1 *Actually* and *as a matter of fact*

> I'm going to stay with someone I know in Paris. *Actually*, he's my cousin. (Adding precise information; we could also use *as a matter of fact* here.)
> A I thought Simon had a degree in languages.
> B *Actually*, he didn't go to university. He learnt Japanese when he worked in Tokyo. (Correcting wrong information; we could also use *as a matter of fact* here.)
> A I didn't like the singer very much.
> B *Actually*, I thought she was excellent. (Disagreeing about an opinion; *as a matter of fact* would sound rather strong here.)
> A Have you cleaned your room yet?
> B *Actually*, I was meaning to do it this afternoon. (Admitting something embarrassing; *as a matter of fact* could sound rather aggressive here.)
>
> **Notes**
> 1 *Actually* is used especially in speech, (a) when we want to ADD EXACT DETAILS to something we have just said, (b) to SOFTEN A REPLY, when we disagree with someone, correct someone, or admit something embarrassing.
> 2 *As a matter of fact* can be used in speech **and** writing, in the same way as *actually*, especially when dealing with FACTS. However, it can sound too strong in matters of opinion or in an embarrassing situation.

Insert *actually* in the sentences and conversations below. Draw a line (/) to show where it should go. Alter punctuation as necessary. Write the changes above the sentences.

1  I bought these shoes in a shop in the High Street. / It's that shop that
Actually, it's
opened last week, right on the corner. It has a very nice range.

2  JOHN: I'm going home now. Would you like a lift?

SUE: I'm not leaving just yet. I've got some work to finish. Thanks, though.

3   ALAN: I admired the Prime Minister's speech on television. Didn't you?

BOB: I found it extremely depressing.

4  MIGOUMI: Let's go for a swim after the lesson this afternoon.

KAORO: I can't swim.

5  Fleming was the first person to notice the effects of penicillin. He discovered the effects by accident. Then later, he discovered what caused these effects.

6  I'm glad Williams is leaving the company. He never seemed particularly good at his job. I heard he only got the job because he's a friend of the boss.

In which sentences could you use *as a matter of fact* instead of *actually*? _____

2 Mixed 'reality' forms, units 16 and 17

Choose the correct form in the sentences below. Sometimes **both** forms are possible.

1 A Did you have a good holiday in Scotland?

  B *In fact*, / *Actually*, we never went to Scotland. We got as far as the Lake District, then we came home.

2 The sales of LPs have declined at the expense of CDs. *Indeed*, / *In fact*, production of classical LPs has ceased entirely.

3 Hodgeson was said to be a fine musician, *and indeed* / *and actually* he had an excellent voice, though I never heard him play an instrument.

4 A How do you like my new jacket?

  B *Actually*, / *Indeed*, it doesn't suit you very well.

5 A Do you think we should buy a 386 computer?

  B *Actually*, / *As a matter of fact*, there's no advantage in getting a 386. The 486 models have come down in price, and they give more speed and power.

6 Everyone thought Stevens had the potential to become a great athlete, *but in fact*, / *and indeed* he never fulfilled the promise he had shown.

18 Exemplification and summation: *For example, for instance, all in all, in short*

1 Exemplification: *For example* and *for instance*

> Geniuses can be very unpleasant as people. *For example,* /*For instance*, Gesualdo, the sixteenth-century Italian composer, was a murderer. (The second sentence provides an EXAMPLE of the first sentence.)
> **Compare:**
> There have been many unpleasant geniuses, *e.g.* the Italian composer Gesualdo. (We can use *e.g.* with a noun phrase, but not to begin a sentence.)

Some of the sentences below are wrong because they do not begin with the correct linker. Find the incorrect sentences and insert a more suitable linker.

1 Pacifica has devalued its currency. ~~For example~~, it will be easier for Pacifica to sell its goods abroad.
   As a result,

2 As Diana's manager, I have to say that she is not at all reliable. For instance, she arrived an hour late yesterday.

3 New technology can lead to a loss of jobs. E.g. a lot of jobs have disappeared through the use of computers.

4 Your essay is excellent. For example, it's the best essay I have read this year.

5 If you receive the document, please send me a copy as quickly as possible. For example, you could send one by fax.

6 It's no use complaining about the job. Nobody would listen to me. For example, I'm starting a new job next month.

2 Summation: *All in all* and *in short*

> He was a kind husband and father, generous to friends, considerate to strangers, and forgiving to enemies. *All in all,* / *In short*, he was a good man.
> (*All in all,* / *In short*, used to SUM UP points already made.)

How could you sum up the ideas below? Use the sentences in the box and *all in all / in short*. Write the beginning of each summing up and a letter from the box.

> A the company's prospects for the coming year are excellent.
> B our tour of Australia was a disaster.
> C she is the best person for the job.
> D he had a miserable childhood.
> E it will cost thousands of pounds to put the house in order.

1 Elizabeth is experienced, good at communicating and highly qualified. <u>All in all (C)</u>

2 Our best players had to go home because of injury and we lost every match. _____

3 Our profits are up, our order book is full, and we have first-class managers. _____

4 His father beat him, his mother died young, and he hated his school. _____

5 The roof leaks, the window frames are rotten and there is no electricity. _____

3 Mixed exemplification and summation forms

Read the sentences below and decide on a suitable order. Before which sentence would you put the linker *for example / for instance* or *all in all / in short*? Read out the complete sentences.

1 (a) You could learn ten new words every day.
 (b) There are various steps you could take to improve your English.

   Order <u> b-a </u> ; linker before <u> (a) For instance </u>

2 (a) We couldn't do without her.
 (b) She's efficient, a good organiser and good at handling people.

   Order _____ ; linker before _____

3 (a) A few mammals have characteristics of birds and reptiles.
 (b) The duck-billed platypus lays eggs.

   Order _____ ; linker before _____

4 (a) Sea City is hot, ugly, smelly and violent.
 (b) It's a place to avoid.

   Order _____ ; linker before _____

5 (a) Some of the expressions taught in books are old-fashioned.
 (b) You are unlikely to hear anyone say 'It's raining cats and dogs'.

   Order _____ ; linker before _____

19 Organisation and narrative linkers: *Firstly, at first; finally, at last;* etc.

1 *Firstly* versus *at first*

> *Firstly,* I would like to deal with the present situation. Then I will deal with our future plans. (*Firstly* is used to show how you are organising points. It is an ORGANISATION linker.)
>
> *At first* our experiments were unsuccessful, but gradually we began to get some useful results. (*At first* is used in describing the order of events in a story or report. It is a NARRATIVE linker.)

Insert *firstly* or *at first* in the sentences below. Draw a line (/) to show where the words should go. Alter punctuation as necessary. Write the changes above the sentences.

1 *At first,*
   /I didn't enjoy the work. It took me a long time to get used to it.

2 There are several reasons why you should choose Sue for the job. She is extremely well qualified. Moreover, she has the necessary experience.

3 (*to an apprentice in a workshop*) Let me look at your work. Mm. It isn't bad, but there are still some faults. You haven't tightened these screws. Can you see them? And also, you've cut these wires too short . . .

4 We shall launch our new models next week. They'll only be available in the London stores, but eventually they'll be sold throughout the country.

5 The company has made mistakes. It should have invested in new technology. Furthermore, it should not have closed down its Atlantica factory.

6 Much research has been carried out on the disease. It was thought that chemical agents were responsible. It is now known to be caused by a virus.

2 More organisation and narrative linkers

Organisation linkers: *First of all, secondly, finally*

> *First of all,* (= *firstly*) I shall show that Frank Martin is innocent of the crime he is accused of. *Secondly,* I shall show why the crime was committed.
>
> *Finally,* I shall name the real criminal.

Narrative linkers: *Finally, at last, in the end, at the start, at the end*

Finally, we produced a sales plan which everyone accepted. (*Finally* can be used both as a narrative linker and an organisation linker.)

At last, after travelling half-way round the world, we managed to interview the head of the company. (*At last* as a narrative linker in a report of events; often used for success after many difficulties.)

For weeks we tried to get in touch with him, but without success. *In the end*, we gave up. (*In the end* as a narrative linker to report something that happened after time or effort. It may not be the result you wanted.)

At the start, the hero is rich and successful. *At the end*, everything has gone wrong. (*At the start / at the end* are narrative linkers used when describing a film/book/play.)

(Mixed organisation and narrative forms) Fiona Brayne, a romantic novelist, is writing a letter to her publisher. Complete the letter with suitable linkers.

---

¹ __Firstly__ , I'd just like to say that I found our meeting very useful, and the lunch was delicious! Unfortunately, when I got to the station I discovered I had missed the last train home. ²_____ , after many inquiries, I decided to take a train to Ipswich and go on from there by taxi – a distance of 20 miles!

³_____ , I'll give you my reactions to your suggestions for *Sad Heart*. ⁴ _____ I wasn't keen on your idea of making the main character an older woman, but now I see how it might work. How about this? ⁵_____ she's shown to be disappointed and uncertain because of the failures in her life, but the story describes how her life goes in new directions. ⁶_____ , she knows who she is, and is ready for new challenges.

⁷_____ , I'd like to clear up one point. I think you said that the royalty would rise to 15% on sales above 10,000. Can you confirm this?

Yours

Fiona Brayne

PS ⁸_____ I've abandoned my dear old typewriter and joined the twentieth century! This letter is written on my new word processor – not so many typing errors for you to correct.

---

20 Addition: *In addition to, besides, as well as*

All the linkers in this section, units 20–25, are phrase linkers.

1 *In addition to* versus *besides* and *as well as*

In addition to fruit, chimpanzees occasionally eat meat. (*In addition to* sounds rather formal, technical or scientific; it suggests an EXACT total.)

What languages do you know *besides* English? (*Besides* is more 'everyday' than *in addition to*; it does not give the idea of counting an exact total.)

We should invite Steve *as well as* Tom. (*As well as* expresses addition in a very general way; it suggests 'equally with' or 'in the same way as'.)

Notes
1 All three expressions often come before an *-ing* form:
In addition to giv*ing* an introduction to computers, the course also provides practical experience. (rather formal sentence)
Besides play*ing* football, he is good at golf. (more 'everyday')
As well as study*ing*, take time to relax. (*As well as* = 'equally with'.)
2 *As well as* can also come before adjectives and prepositions:
She was kind *as well as* sensible. (before adjective)
The snow fell on low ground *as well as on* the mountains. (before preposition)

Complete the sentences below by adding *in addition to*, *besides* or *as well as*. More than one answer may be possible. Draw a line (/) to show where the words should go.

in addition to

1 He owns a flat in London /his castles in Scotland and Ireland, so that makes three residences altogether.

2 (*a teacher makes a suggestion*) checking the students' grammar you should listen to their pronunciation.

3 her reputation as a novelist she is also highly regarded as a poet.

4 You may take one more course the courses you have already enrolled for.

5 (*a doctor speaks*) giving you an X-ray we're going to do a blood test.

6 People can get pleasure from pop music from classical music.

7 We ought to be forgiving to our enemies helpful to our friends.

8 (*a question at a job interview*) Have you had any other experience the job you had in Hong Kong?

9 (*a budget speech*) We shall save £5 billion by cutting government expenditure the £7.5 billion which we shall raise through increases in taxation.

2 *In addition to* versus *in addition*; *as well as* versus *as well*

> *In addition to* a profitable hotel business he owns several restaurants.
>
> He has a profitable hotel business. *In addition*, he owns several restaurants.
>
> *As well as* my brothers and sisters, some of my cousins came to the wedding.
>
> My brothers and sisters came to the wedding. Some of my cousins came *as well*.

Note
In addition to and *as well as* go with phrases and *-ing* forms. *In addition* and *as well* go with complete sentences (they are across-sentence linkers). Notice that *in addition* usually comes at the beginning of a sentence. *As well* nearly always comes at the end.

Rewrite the sentences below using the form given in brackets.

1 John got US dollars for the journey. He also got travellers' cheques.

   (a) <u>John got US dollars for the journey. In addition, he</u>
       <u>got travellers' cheques.</u>   (in addition)

   (b) _____ (in addition to)

2 She is efficient. She is also extremely clever.

   (a) _____ (as well)

   (b) _____ (as well as)

3 There are courses in computing. A business course is also on offer.

   (a) _____ (in addition to)

   (b) _____ (in addition)

4 The exhibition contained oil paintings. It also showed some water-colours.

   (a) _____ (as well as)

   (b) _____ (as well)

5 We shall provide hotel accommodation. We shall also cover travel expenses.

   (a) _____ (in addition)

   (b) _____ (in addition to)

6 He is endangering his own life. He is also putting others in danger.

   (a) _____ (as well)

   (b) _____ (as well as)

21 Contrast: *In spite of / despite* (versus *although*)

1 *In spite of* and *despite*

> *In spite of* a bad cold, she sang brilliantly. (= The fact that she sang well is surprising, given the fact that she had a bad cold.)
>
> *In spite of* play*ing* well, we lost the match. (*In spite of* before *-ing* form.)
>
> **Notes**
> 1 *In spite of* is used before a fact which makes the rest of the sentence seem surprising by contrast. It can come before a noun phrase, or an *-ing* form.
> 2 *Despite* has the same meaning as *in spite of*, but sounds more formal or literary. We could use *despite* in the example sentences:
>   *Despite* a bad cold, . . .
>   *Despite* play*ing* well, . . .
> 3 We could also write the example sentences the opposite way round:
>   She sang brilliantly, *in spite of* a bad cold.
>   We lost the match, *in spite of* play*ing* well.

Rewrite these notes using *in spite of* and *despite*. Sometimes an *-ing* form is required.

1 he was never satisfied / he was one of the richest men in the world
   <u>He was never satisfied, despite being one of the richest men in the world.</u>

2 we arrived on time / the heavy traffic on the motorway
   _____

3 our team lost two early goals / our team won comfortably in the end
   _____

4 our present economic difficulties / the company should recover next year
   _____

5 the police chief fought against the Mafia / he received death threats
   _____

6 she became president of the company / widespread prejudice against women
   _____

7 Joe did not become wealthy / he worked hard all his life
   _____

8 Relatively few buildings were damaged / the severity of the earthquake

_____

9 Jill is back at work / she has just had a baby

_____

2 ***In spite of* versus *although***

> *In spite of* **many failures**, he did not give up. (Many failures = noun phrase.)
>
> *In spite of* **failing** many times, he did not give up. (Failing = *-ing* form.)
> **Compare:**
> *Although* he failed many times, he did not give up. (*Although* comes before a clause with the subject *he* and the verb *failed*.)
>
> **Note**
> *In spite of* has the same meaning as *although*, but *although* comes before a complete clause containing a subject and a verb. *In spite of* **cannot** come before a clause. It **must** come before a noun phrase or an *-ing* form.

Read the news items below. Choose between *although* and *in spite of* (or *despite*).

1 The government has announced that *although / in spite of* the sharp
   downturn in economic activity, it will not abandon its anti-inflation policy.
   Although / in spite of unemployment increased by 250,000 last month,
   tight control of government spending is seen as the key to recovery.

2 (*reviewing a motor show*) *Although / In spite of* the new Splendido XL2
   contains many improvements, the price remains the same as for the XL1.
   At £24,000, the car represents excellent value, *although / despite* it is
   obviously not a vehicle for the average motorist.

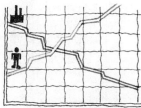

3 Famines and food shortages have increased in the Third World, *despite /
   although* improved methods of agriculture. Moreover, *in spite of / although*
   there is actually a surplus of some types of food in Western Europe and
   the USA, much of this food is wasted, or even destroyed.

4 (*travel report*) *Despite/Although* widespread fog tonight, there are no
   reports of any problems at the airports. However, *although / in spite of*
   warning lights on the M1 motorway, the police are still reporting problems
   with motorists driving too close to the car in front.

22 Reason: *Because of* (versus *because*)

1 Because of

> We came home *because of* the rain. (The rain is the reason for coming home. This sentence might occur in conversation.)
>
> *Because of* the warmer climate in the south of the country, agriculture is more successful in that region. (The warmer climate is the reason for success. This sentence might occur in formal writing.)

> **Note**
> *Because of* is used before a noun phrase which expresses a REASON for something. It can be used both in conversation and writing.

General Worthington was a famous hero in Victorian times.
Join the events in his life and the reasons for them.
Write sentences with *because of* underneath.

Events	Reasons
1 He had a strict upbringing	a a desire for adventure.
2 He won a scholarship to a famous school	b his qualities of leadership.
3 The other boys teased him	c ill-health.
4 He wanted to join the army	d his parents' religious beliefs.
5 At first the army would not take him	e bravery in battle.
6 He became a successful commander	f his abilities in maths and sport.
7 He was given many medals	g his strange regional accent.
8 He retired from the army at 45	h his age.

1 _____

2 _____

3 _____

4 _____

5 _____

6 _____

7 _____

8 _____

2 *Because of* versus *because*

> We turned back *because of* the floods on the road. (*The floods on the road* is a noun phrase.)
> **Compare:**
> We turned back *because* the roads were flooded. (*Because* is a WITHIN-SENTENCE LINKER; *the roads were flooded* is a clause containing a subject and a verb.)
>
> **Note**
> *Because of* is a PHRASE LINKER; it comes before a noun phrase. *Because* is a WITHIN-SENTENCE LINKER; it comes before a clause.

Change 'because of' sentences to 'because' sentences, and vice versa.

1 Because of the extreme difficulty of the exam, many students failed.
   <u>Many students failed because the exam was so difficult.</u>

2 Because Joan worked hard she soon became indispensable to the company.
   _____

3 Tim has to go to the dentist because of an infected tooth.
   _____

4 Because of Joy's foolish behaviour everyone in the class was punished.
   _____

5 The motorist was fined £100 because he drove dangerously.
   _____

6 Alice has joined a choir because of her love of singing.
   _____

3 Underline the correct forms in the dialogues below.

1 A Why are you opening the windows?
   B *Because / Because of* I smell gas.

2 A Is Brian leaving the company *because of / because* his age?
   B No. It's *because of / because* he wants to move back to head office.

3 A I'm very grateful to you. It's *because / because of* your help that
      I managed to do the job. I couldn't have done it on my own.
   B That's OK. It's just *because of / because* you're new here that
      everything seems so confusing. You'll soon get used to the system.

23 Reason: *As a result of / because of; owing to / due to*

1 *As a result of* (versus *because of*)

He lost his memory *as a result of* a severe blow on the head. (The loss of memory is the DIRECT result of a particular, physical event.)

He lost his memory *as a result of* receiving a severe blow. (*As a result of* before an *-ing* form.)

He stopped teaching *because of* all the violence in the school. (*Because of* with something that leads to a decision.)

Notes
1 *As a result of* suggests that one event is the single, DIRECT (often physical) cause of another. *Because of* suggests a LESS DIRECT connection – for example, someone looks at a situation, makes a mental judgment, and then takes action.
2 We can use *as a result of* but not *because of* before an *-ing* form.

Which do you think is better in these sentences – *because of* or *as a result of*?

1 A Why did you decide to leave the company?

   B *Because of / As a result of* new management policies which I totally disagreed with.

2 I was made redundant *as a result of / because of* company reorganisation.

3 The home team scored in the last minute *as a result of / because of* an error by the opposing goalkeeper.

4 *Because of / As a result of* the opposing team's superior attacking skills, we worked out a clever defensive plan.

5 Sea levels may rise *as a result of / because of* global warming.

6 Governments may take measures to limit CO_2 emissions *because of / as a result of* the dangers of global warming.

7 I get depressed *as a result of / because of* all the unhappiness in the world.

8 We are getting a 10% pay rise immediately *because of / as a result of* the recent wage agreement.

9 *As a result of / Because of* eating well, she soon regained her strength.

10 *Because of / As a result of* the excellent food at the hotel, she booked a holiday there for the following year.

11 Joe met his wife *as a result of / because of* an advertisement he inserted in a newspaper.

2   *Owing to* versus *due to*

> The factory had to close *owing to* a lack of orders. (Some people might use *due to* in this sentence, but it is better not to use *due to* except after the verb *be*, as in the sentence below.)
>
> The closure of the factory **was** *due to* a lack of orders. (*Due to* after the verb *be*; we **cannot** use *owing to* in this sentence.)
>
> **Notes**
> 1 *Owing to* means the same as *because of*. It sounds rather formal or official. It often occurs in writing (e.g. newspaper articles, reports).
> 2 Some people use *due to* in the same way as *owing to*. However, in 'correct' writing we only use *due to* after a form of *be* (*is, are, was, were*, etc.). We **cannot** use *owing to* after *be*.

Read these sentences about 'sounds'. Choose *due to* or *owing to*, following the guidance in the notes above.

1

Owing to / Due to the noise a drill makes, ear protection is necessary.

2

Increasing deafness among young people may be *owing to / due to* their exposure to rock music, say scientists.

3

Some language teachers find classical music useful in their lessons, *owing to / due to* its relaxing effect.

4

Many quarrels between neighbours are *owing to / due to* noisy parties.

5

Many airports prohibit night take-offs *due to / owing to* the problem of aircraft noise.

6

If you come from a city, you may find it hard to sleep in the country *owing to / due to* the silence.

24 Clarification: *Namely, i.e., for example / e.g., such as, including, especially*

1 *Namely* versus *i.e.*

	DESCRIPTIVE PHRASE	EXACT WORD
Professor Fry is studying	**the largest aquatic mammal**	*namely* **the Blue Whale**.
	EXACT WORD	DESCRIPTIVE PHRASE
Professor Fry is studying	**the Blue Whale,**	*i.e.* **the largest aquatic mammal**.

Notes

1 *Namely* comes after a DESCRIPTIVE PHRASE for an item, before the EXACT WORD.

2 *i.e.* can be used the **opposite** way from *namely*. It often comes **after** THE EXACT WORD for an item, and **before** a DESCRIPTIVE PHRASE. It can be read aloud as 'that is' or 'that is to say' as well as 'eye-ee'.

3 Both *namely* and *i.e.* tend to be used after long phrases. After short phrases a comma or dash may be enough, without any linking word.

Insert *namely* or *i.e.* in the sentences below, following the guidance in the notes above. Draw a line (/) to show where the word should go.

1 The prime minister was educated at one of the most famous
    namely
  public schools in England, / Eton.

2 She dedicated her last book to 'Dear Bill, who made it all possible',
  the cousin who had helped her when she was a young writer.

3 The competition to stage the Olympics was closely fought between
  two great Latin American cities, Buenos Aires and Rio de Janeiro.

4 There was one make of computer which seemed to offer particularly
  good value for money on the basis of our tests, the Tranox 486.

5 For his birthday Tom received a pair of blue and white woollen socks
  knitted by his aunt, a present he had no use for whatsoever.

6 There was only one person who was against the idea, myself.

7 There may be other planets in the universe like Earth, planets with
  oxygen and water.

2 For example / e.g., such as, including, especially

Certain mammals have adapted to living in water, *for example / e.g.* the dolphin and the whale. (*For example* before examples; comma before *for example*.)

Mammals *such as* the dolphin and the whale have adapted to living in water. (*Such as* = 'with the characteristics of'; no comma before or after it.)

In the twenty-first century spaceships will visit all the planets, *including* Pluto. (= Pluto is among the group of planets which spaceships will visit.)

Professor Fry has studied various aquatic mammals, *especially* whales and dolphins. (His studies on other aquatic mammals are not so important.)

(Mixed forms) Choose suitable forms to complete the passage below. Note that punctuation is sometimes important in choosing an answer.

In the twenty-first century, we shall see a great increase in the use of alternative energy sources, [1] *especially / such as* wind and water power. Several states in the USA already use wind power, [2] *for example / namely* California, where huge 'wind farms' have been constructed ([3] *i.e. / e.g.* power stations consisting of many windmills linked together in series). Water power, too, is already an important source of electricity in countries with plentiful rivers and lakes [4] *such as / for example* Norway.

Solar energy is another energy source which will be widely used in areas with plenty of sunshine [5] *such as / i.e.* Egypt and the countries of North Africa. Solar energy may even make a contribution in regions with cool climates, [6] *namely/including* the countries of northern Europe. France has one particularly important solar energy research facility, [7] *especially/namely* the solar generator at Font Romeu, in the Pyrenees.

By contrast, the use of nuclear power may diminish. Problems with nuclear safety, [8] *especially / such as* the accident at Chernobyl, have made governments less willing to invest in nuclear power stations. However, scientists are working to produce energy safely from nuclear 'fusion', [9] *i.e./including* a technique in which atoms are joined together. This could replace the present basis of nuclear power, [10] *namely/ especially* nuclear 'fission', in which atoms are split apart.

25 Time: *During* (versus *while* and *meanwhile*)

1 *During*

> We went swimming every day *during* the summer. (= all through the summer)
>
> He died *during* the night. (= at a particular moment in the night)
>
> **Note**
> *During* means (a) all through a period of time, (b) at a moment within a period of time. It is a PHRASE LINKER, used before a noun phrase.

In which of the sentences below could you insert *during*? Where would you insert it? (Notice that you cannot use *during* in **every** sentence.)

1 We hope you enjoy yourselves / ^{during} your stay with us. ✔

2 Do you know the song, 'Whistle you work?' _____

3 One of our players was injured the match and had to leave the field. _____

4 John was comforted by many expressions of sympathy his long illness. _____

5 I'll phone my wife the coffee break. _____

6 The director spoke to the sales representatives he was at the conference. _____

2 *While* versus *during*

> They arrived *while* we were having dinner. (*While* before the clause we *were having dinner*.)
>
> *While* having dinner, we heard their car. (*While* before an *-ing* form; short for 'while we were having dinner'.)
>
> They arrived *during* dinner. (*During* before the noun *dinner*.)
>
> **Notes**
> *While* comes before a CLAUSE or an *-ing* form.
> *During* comes before a NOUN PHRASE.

Complete the following passage with *during* or *while*. It comes from a story about an industrial dispute.

Riley was back. He came up to Farrell [1] _during_ the break.

'You've been spreading rumours about me [2] _____ I've been in jail,' he said angrily. 'You said that [3] _____ the strike I reported to the managers every day. You said that [4] _____ men were going hungry I was getting money from the company – a secret deal, cash in little brown envelopes.'

[5] _____ addressing Farrell, Riley had become more and more agitated. He seemed about to explode. Farrell had heard that once, [6] _____ an earlier dispute, Riley had knocked a man out. It was time to calm things down.

'Look, Riley, I heard the rumours but I didn't start them. I believe that someone was spying on us [7] _____ the strike was on, but I know it wasn't you. Of course, [8] _____ you were away, a lot of strange stories were going around. But now we have to clear things up. Tonight we're going to have a vote on whether to take further action. [9] _____ the meeting, I'm going to produce facts to show who the spy really was.'

3   *Meanwhile* versus *while* and *during*

> They'll be here soon. *Meanwhile*, let's have coffee. (*Meanwhile* = 'during this period of time'.)
>
> My brother was having a good time with his friends. *Meanwhile*, I was sitting at home and studying. (*Meanwhile* = 'while all this was going on'.)
> **Compare:**
> My brother was having a good time *while* I was sitting at home.
> My brother had a good time *during* the holidays.
>
> **Note**
> *Meanwhile* is an ACROSS-SENTENCE LINKER, usually with a comma after it.

Read the sentences below. Choose the correct form.

1 The town carnival was reaching a climax. *Meanwhile,*/*While* the robbers were tunnelling their their way into the bank.

2 One of the wedding guests fainted *during*/*meanwhile* the wedding ceremony.

3 We'll wait for the others to arrive. *During*/*Meanwhile*, I'll hand out some brochures.

4 (*old Latin song*) 'Let's have a good time *meanwhile*/*while* we are young – soon the earth will cover us.'

5 (*walkers trapped in a snowstorm*) 'The rescue party will reach us soon. *Meanwhile,*/*While* let's try to build a shelter.'

26 Review 1: Linkers from sections 1 and 2

1 Complete the passages below using words from the list underneath.

The process of becoming an adult is important in the life of any human being. [1] ___Thus___ , most human societies mark the change from child to adult in some way, often with special 'initiation ceremonies'.

   [2] _____ both sexes may undergo initiation ceremonies, in societies where males are dominant, they are particularly important for boys. [3] _____ , a boy may not be considered a real 'man' [4] _____ he can show great qualities of endurance. [5] _____ he may have to endure having his thumb nails torn out, [6] _____ he might have some teeth removed. Sometimes there is a space of years between initiation ceremonies, [7] _____ it is not unusual for a man to be over thirty [8] _____ he becomes a full 'adult'.

   In some societies age and status are indicated by a person's clothes. [9] _____ , in England up to about 1960, boys wore short trousers [10] _____ they were well into their teens. Being allowed to wear long trousers was [11] _____ a clear sign that you were no longer a child. [12] _____ , even when you were allowed to dress in an 'adult' way, you would not be considered a full 'adult', [13] _____ you would not have the right to vote, to drive a car, to marry without your parents' consent, etc.

1 a) For example b) Thus c) Instead

2 a) Although b) But c) Incidentally

3 a) At least b) Firstly c) Indeed

4 a) unless b) because c) provided

5 a) At least b) In other words c) For example

6 a) or b) whereas c) since

7 a) but b) at last c) so

8 a) before b) until c) while

9 a) All in all b) As a matter of fact
   c) For instance

10 a) until b) as c) unless

11 a) firstly b) in any case c) therefore

12 a) On the other hand b) Incidentally

13 a) before b) in case c) since

56

2 Mrs Black is a community health worker. She is giving a talk to a group of parents. Complete her talk using the linkers in the boxes before each section.

> as a matter of fact   so   at first   because   by the way
>
> firstly   but   the thing is   whereas

Good morning. [1] __At first__   when I came in this morning I thought I would talk about childhood illnesses, [2] _____ then I was asked to say something about 'safety in the home', [3] _____ I'll begin with that.

[4] _____ , I'll say a few general words. [5] _____ , people don't realise that homes are dangerous places. [6] _____ , the statistics show that more accidents occur in the home than any other single location. It's curious isn't it? [7] _____ the dangers on the roads and in factories are obvious, the dangers in the home just aren't understood.

[8] _____ , I just read in the paper this morning a good example of this – a five-year-old boy who had to be rushed to hospital [9] _____ he pulled a boiling kettle off a stove and burnt himself – did any of you read that?

> in case   for example   all in all   anyway   on the contrary
>
> provided   in other words   alternatively   in addition   in fact

[10] _____ , as I was saying, we have to become aware of the dangers. Let's consider the dangers of poisoning. Some people think that [11] _____ they store things like bleach and household cleaners out of sight of children, everything will be all right, and they forget that children love to explore and taste everything. Remember, access by children must be prevented. [12] _____ , keep substances out of children's reach. [13] _____ you could keep them in a locked cupboard. [14] _____ , you could store them on a high shelf.

[15] _____ , you should take care with any medicines that are in the house. You shouldn't take pills in front of children, [16] _____ they think they are something nice to eat, like sweets. [17] _____ you shouldn't ask your doctor for sweet tasting medicine at all. [18] _____ , it's better to get medicine that tastes like 'real' medicine. [19] _____ , you should treat **all** powders, liquids and pills in the house with the greatest respect.

27 Review 2: Linkers from sections 2 and 3

1 Complete the essay about gold. Choose suitable linkers from the words in italics. (Note: Pay attention to the capital letters at the beginning of some words.)

During / At last / Meanwhile / While / In any case / namely / including / Incidentally

Gold! The early settlers in America had always hoped to find it. [1] __At last__ · it was discovered in California, in 1849. [2] _____ the years that followed, thousands of people rushed to the diggings. [3] _____ , the gold rush of 1849 produced one of the most famous of all American songs, [4] _____ 'Clementine'.

At the end/including/In spite of/i.e./namely/but in fact/In the end/In addition to

[5] _____ all the difficulties they had to undergo, [6] _____ starvation and disease, the 'prospectors' ([7] _____ gold miners and gold panners) kept up their desperate search. Their numbers were huge, [8] _____ very few of them ever 'struck it rich'. [9] _____ , most of them had to give up and go back home.

due to / Indeed / Moreover / as well as / However / For example / owing to / especially / By contrast

Gold has always been a scarce metal. [10] _____ , all the gold ever produced would only fill the space of a large house. [11] _____ , it is a metal with certain extremely desirable characteristics. [12] _____ , it can easily be hammered into different shapes, [13] _____ its extreme softness. [14] _____ , it can be drawn into a wire, with one gram of metal stretching to a length of nearly three kilometres. Its attractiveness to jewellers and metal workers is [15] _____ these qualities, [16] _____ the fact that gold is remarkably resistant to corrosion.

especially / such as / In addition to / hence / In short / because of / despite / For instance

[17] _____ its use in jewellery, gold has found other, more practical applications. [18] _____ , gold is an excellent conductor of electricity and [19] _____ extremely useful in the electronics industry, for items [20] _____ electrical contacts. Gold even has medical uses, being given as a treatment for certain diseases, [21] _____ arthritis.

besides/however/Nevertheless/at least/in other words/e.g./namely/therefore

Perhaps the most important use of gold, [22] _____ , is in its connection with money. Gold is used for coinage; [23] _____ it was formerly used in this way, and is still used to make coins for special occasions, [24] _____ the coronation of a king or queen. Nowadays, gold coins do not enter general circulation. [25] _____ , gold is still used by countries to store their wealth. It is [26] _____ of great importance.

2 Choose the correct forms in this lecture about 'creatures great and small'.

I want you to think of two particular types of animal, [1]*namely/including* an elephant and a mouse. What's the difference between them? Well, you could say, 'an elephant is bigger than a mouse', [2]*but in fact / and indeed* you'd be right. An elephant weighs 10 tonnes. [3]*By contrast / Conversely* a mouse is absolutely minute – no more than a few grams in weight. [4]*In any case / However*, I'm going to tell you that in one respect, a mouse is 'bigger' than an elephant, [5]*or rather / but in fact* it has 'more' of something, if you make the proper comparison.

[6]*First of all / At first*, imagine that you could measure the complete surface area of an elephant, and then the complete surface area of a mouse. [7]*Actually/Besides*, that would be a difficult thing to do, wouldn't it? [8]*Anyway / In short*, just imagine it – you measure the total area in square centimetres. [9]*In the end / Secondly*, imagine that you could measure the volume of each animal, [10]*i.e./namely* the amount of space it takes up. OK?

Now imagine that you divide the surface area of each animal by its volume. Amazingly, the answer will be higher for the mouse than for the elephant. [11]*In other words / Otherwise*, a mouse has a greater surface area – more skin if you like – than an elephant, in relation to its volume.

[12]*Hence/Actually*, this demonstrates a basic biological fact, [13]*namely / such as* that the bigger the animal, the smaller its relative surface area. This is important for factors [14]*such as / for example* temperature control. [15]*In any case / The thing is*, large animals, with a lower relative surface area, preserve their body heat very well, but may have difficulty in getting rid of heat. [16]*Hence / By the way*, animals such as elephants need special ways of getting rid of excess heat – they lose heat by flapping their large ears, or they spray themselves with water, etc. [17]*On the other hand / Otherwise* they would be in danger of overheating.

[18]*Conversely/Otherwise*, small animals have the problem of keeping their temperature high. Think of an animal such as a mouse or a shrew. It loses a great deal of its body heat to its surroundings. [19]*Consequently / By contrast*, it constantly seeks out sources of energy – [20]*in other words / including* it spends most of its life trying to find things to eat.

28 Review 3: Linkers from all sections

Choose the correct form.

1 I stood on a chair _____ I could reach the high shelf.
    a) so that   b) therefore   c) because   d) until

2 _____ their parents' opposition, Tom and Ann decided to get married.
    a) Although   b) However   c) Despite   d) Owing to

3 _____ my car dates from 1981, yours is brand new.
    a) Nevertheless   b) In spite of   c) Although   d) Whereas

4 _____ I have great respect for him, I don't particularly like him.
    a) Despite   b) Although   c) In fact   d) But

5 Tim isn't suitable for the job. He's too old. _____ , he isn't interested.
    a) Besides   b) In addition to   c) As well as   d) And

6 I'll assume that you're coming _____ I hear from you.
    a) otherwise   b) provided   c) in case   d) unless

7 I haven't had any news of Tim for ages. _____ , do you have his address?
    a) By the way   b) Moreover   c) Besides   d) The thing is

8 _____ there are no more questions to discuss, we can finish the meeting.
    a) As   b) Because   c) So that   d) Unless

9 The efficiency survey gave no useful results, offered no suggestions, and annoyed everyone. _____ , it was a complete waste of time.
    a) Otherwise   b) Incidentally   c) In any case   d) In short

10 He worked for the same company all his life _____ he retired.
    a) before   b) unless   c) finally   d) until

11 _____ my wife, can I bring two more guests to the party?
    a) Moreover   b) Furthermore   c) In addition to   d) As well as

12 Remember to take a key with you _____ you come home late.
    a) in case   b) provided   c) if   d) unless

13 Linkers are quite difficult to learn. _____ , they are worth studying.
    a) In spite of   b) Although   c) In other words   d) Nevertheless

14 I did not support his view. _____ , I disagreed strongly.
    a) On the contrary   b) Otherwise   c) By contrast   d) Conversely

15 Several of our players were injured, _____ the goalkeeper.
    a) especially   b) such as   c) e.g.   d) including

Answer key

A first look at linkers

4 1 although 2 However 3 The thing is 4 also 5 unless 6 during 7 because of
(a) until, unless
(b) however, also, The thing is
(c) during, because of

1 Addition, contrast, alternatives: *And, but, or*

1 1 but 2 or 3 and 4 or

2 1 An earthquake struck South America yesterday and caused some damage.
2 Penicillin was developed in the 1940s and has saved thousands of lives.
3 –
4 The manager invited workers' representatives to the meeting and explained the position to them.
5 Susan and I went on a trip to Romania and saw a lot of interesting sights.
6 –
7 This is a unique area for wildlife and has to be protected.
8 This has many useful features and could become a favourite for many writers.

2 Contrast: *But, although, whereas*

1 1 (a) Sally isn't very tall, but she is good at basketball.
(b) Although Sally isn't very tall, she is good at basketball.
2 (a) Mongolia is a large country but it does not have a large population
(b) Although Mongolia is a large country, it does not have a large population.
3 (a) Jane likes to sing but she is not a very good singer.
(b) Although Jane likes to sing, she is not a very good singer.
4 (a) I did not pay a lot of money for my car, but it runs very well.
(b) Although I did not pay a lot of money for my car, it runs very well.
5 (a) Syntex is a smaller company than Tenbol, but it is more profitable.
(b) Although Syntex is a smaller company than Tenbol, it is more profitable.
6 (a) Van Gogh did not sell any paintings during his lifetime but they are now worth millions.

(b) Although Van Gogh did not sell any paintings during his lifetime, they are now worth millions.
7 (a) We did not play well, but we won the match.
(b) Although we did not play well, we won the match.
8 (a) A lot of novels are published every year, but very few become bestsellers.
(b) Although a lot of novels are published every year, very few become bestsellers.
9 (a) Smallpox has been eradicated, but there remain diseases for which there is no cure.
(b) Although smallpox has been eradicated, there remain diseases for which there is no cure.

2 1–whereas–b 2–although–d 3–although–g 4–whereas–h 5–although–i 6–whereas–a 7–although–a 8–whereas–c 9–whereas–e 10–although–f

3 Reason and purpose: *Because, since, as, so that*

1 1 because 2 as 3 Because/As 4 Since/As 5 Because 6 as/because 7 because 8 because 9 because 10 because 11 since/because

2 1 (a) Dave is driving fast so that he'll arrive on time.
(b) Dave is driving fast because he's late.
2 (a) Louise wore a pink dress so that Ann would recognise her at the airport.
(b) Louise wore a pink dress because it was her favourite colour.
3 (a) Ben has put nets on the window so that the mosquitoes can't come in.
(b) Ben has put nets on the window because there are so many insects.
4 (a) Antoine has bought a computer so that he can play games on it.
(b) Antoine has bought a computer because he needs it for his work.
5 (a) Nora eats green vegetables so that she can get enough vitamins.
(b) Nora eats green vegetables because they're good for her health.

4 Result: *So* (versus *so that, because*, etc.)

1 1 As we had finished our work we went home.

2 Lise and Colin have got engaged, so they're having a party.
3 This is the tourist season, so accommodation may be expensive.
4 She learnt Italian because she wanted to read Dante in the original language.
5 I don't like disco music, so I'm not going to the disco.
6 Since you know what is in the letter, I won't read it to you.
7 As I wasn't present when the accident happened, you can't blame me.
8 Meg wasn't invited to the wedding, so she is really angry.
9 Jim bought drinks for everybody because he had won £50 in a lottery.
10 Since we're here, let's enjoy ourselves.

2 1 (a) so that (b) so
2 (a) so (b) so that
3 (a) so that (b) so
4 (a) so (b) so that

3 A 1 because 2 so that 3 As/Since 4 because/since 5 because 6 so
B 7 so that 8 As 9 because 10 as 11 so

5 Time: *While, as, until, before*

1 1 As; opened
2 While; were investigating
3 while/as; rot / are rotting
4 While; was sailing
5 as; began
6 As; moved
7 as/while; drive / are driving
8 while; were staying

2 1 as 2 before 3 until 4 While 5 until 6 before 7 while 8 As 9 As; Before; while; before; until; while

6 Condition: *If, provided (that), in case, if not, unless*

1 1 provided 2 in case 3 If 4 if/provided 5 If 6 in case 7 in case 8 provided 9 provided 10 in case

2 1 Both 2 b 3 a 4 a 5 Both 6 a 7 a 8 a

7 Addition: *Also, moreover, in addition, besides*

1 1 You can also get them by mail order.
2 He had also been a fine athlete in his youth.
3 Emergency lighting should also be checked regularly.

4 He also has a number of more exotic creatures.
5 She is also going to present the prizes.
6 He also runs an oil company.
7 The closeness of the house to the city also suited them.

2 1 In addition 2 also 3 Moreover
4 Besides 5 also 6 Besides 7 In addition 8 Moreover

8 Contrast: *However, nevertheless*

1 1 (a) The Ancient Greeks discovered steam power. However, they did not use it industrially.
  (b) The Ancient Greeks discovered steam power. They did not, however, use it industrially.
2 (a) My sister eats meat. However, my brother is a strict vegetarian.
  (b) My sister eats meat. My brother, however, is a strict vegetarian.
3 (a) Early computers took up whole rooms. However, modern computers occupy much less space.
  (b) Early computers took up whole rooms. Modern computers, however, occupy much less space.
4 (a) Most snakebites are non-fatal. However, occasionally they cause death.
  (b) Most snakebites are non-fatal. Occasionally, however, they cause death.
5 (a) Some babies walk at nine months. However, in general they walk around thirteen months.
  (b) Some babies walk at nine months. In general, however, they walk around thirteen months.
same people/things: 1, 4, 5
different people/things: 2, 3

2 1 However 2 However
3 nevertheless 4 However
5 nevertheless 6 However
7 However/Nevertheless

9 Contrast and comparison: *On the other hand, by contrast, on the contrary, conversely*

1 1 (a) On the other hand (b) By contrast
2 (a) On the other hand (b) By contrast
3 (a) By contrast (b) On the other hand

4 (a) By contrast (b) On the other hand
5 (a) On the other hand (b) By contrast
6 (a) On the other hand (b) By contrast

2 1 Conversely, only 10% of the lowest group . . .
2 On the contrary, I think he was completely justified in doing so.
3 On the contrary, he's always spoken well of you.
4 Conversely, the percentage of people . . .
5 Conversely, if there are two equal angles . . .
6 On the contrary, applications from . . .

10 Results and conclusions: *Thus, therefore*

1 1 The president was very unpopular. Thus, his resignation did not come as a surprise.
2 The government intends to reduce taxes and thus increase its popularity.
3 There had been riots in the streets. Thus, the army decided to take control.
4 The police fired tear gas and thus managed to disperse the protesters.
5 The government has announced a programme of reform. Thus, it will improve social benefits for the poor.
6 The health minister claimed that great progress had been made. Thus, 240 new hospitals had been built.
7 The opposition parties voted against the proposal and thus prevented it from becoming law.
8 The new minister, Mrs Duras, is energetic. Thus, she will probably adopt new policies.

2 1 Our department does not deal with these matters. We are therefore unable to help.
2 The books you borrowed are overdue. You should therefore return them immediately.
3 I no longer have a car. I therefore wish to cancel my insurance policy.
4 We have received many complaints. We must therefore ask you to reduce the noise level.
5 You are a valued customer. I am therefore sending you our new catalogue.
6 You sent the money on 16th June. Payment therefore arrived several days late.
7 The Newtown branch is unprofitable. The company has therefore decided to close it.

11 Results and conclusions: *Hence, consequently*; mixed reason/result forms

1 1 There is no defect in the fuel system of the car. Hence, the fault appears to lie with the electrical system.
2 Several teachers are ill. Consequently, the school will be closed until further notice.
3 The ship suffered damage in a storm. Consequently, it had to go into port for repairs.
4 There is no evidence of damage to the door. Hence, the thieves must have entered the building through the window.
5 Over 90% of our patients improved after taking the drug. Hence, the drug can be regarded as an effective treatment for the disease.
6 Calcium hydroxide is an alkali. Hence, it reacts with acids to form a salt plus water.
7 The temperature in Saudi Arabia can reach 50°C. Consequently a lot of business is done late in the day.
8 The soldiers in the Pacifican Army were poorly paid. Hence/Consequently morale was extremely low.

2 1 so 2 thus 3 Consequently
4 therefore 5 Thus 6 as
7 hence 8 therefore 9 hence
10 Thus 11 Since

12 Alternatives: *Alternatively, otherwise, instead*

1 1 I hope he drives carefully. Otherwise he may have an accident.
2 If the goods are faulty, we can replace them. Alternatively we can give you a refund.
3 There's a plane tonight. Alternatively you could get one tomorrow morning.
4 Tom will have to work harder. Otherwise he'll fail.
5 We must improve our profits. Otherwise we could go bankrupt.
6 You can buy the car now or alternatively you can pay for it in instalments.

2 1 . . . and instead decided to extend our existing house.
2 . . . in future. Instead they will run on hydrogen.
3 . . . exchange, but instead lost everything.
4 . . . Hong Kong. We send faxes instead.
5 . . . obsolete. Instead, most writing is done on word processors.

3
1 Otherwise 2 instead
3 Alternatively 4 Instead
5 Otherwise 6 alternatively

13 Rephrasing and correcting: *In other words, or rather, at least*

1
1 Or rather
2 At least
3 In other words
4 At least
5 Or rather
6 at least
7 In other words
8 At least
9 at least
10 In other words

14 'Main point' linkers: *Anyway, in any case, the thing is*

1
1 I'm too tired.
2 If a fault should develop, . . .
3 It appears that the technique will play a part in language teaching in future.
4 She won't be at work today.
5 It's getting late.
In any case (not *anyway*) in passages 2 and 3

2
1 The thing is
2 Anyway
3 Anyway
4 The thing is
5 The thing is

15 'Extra point' linkers: *By the way, incidentally*; mixed 'main' and 'extra' forms

1
1 c–a–b; a
2 c–b–a; a
3 a–b–c/a–c–b; b
4 b–a–c; c
5 b–c–a; a

2
1 By the way
2 In any case
3 Incidentally
4 The thing is
5 In any case / Anyway
6 Incidentally
7 The thing is
8 By the way

16 Reality: *(but) in fact, (and) indeed*

1
1 The weatherman had promised sunny weather, but in fact, it rained all day.
2 Dynamo are a very good team. In fact, they are the best team in the country.

3 Research on anti-viral drugs is making good progress. In fact, a cure for many deadly diseases is only a few years away.
4 We expected to reach our destination by midday, but in fact, we arrived even earlier.
5 The expedition hoped to climb the mountain by August, but in fact it was mid-September before they could begin the ascent.

2
1 Indeed, he is the best athlete in these games.
2 The newspapers praised him highly, and indeed he did an excellent job.
3 no change
4 Indeed, the publishers considered dropping it from their list.
5 no change

3
1 a 2 a 3 b 4 a

17 Reality: *Actually, as a matter of fact*; mixed 'reality' forms

1
1 Actually, it's that shop that opened last week, . . .
2 Actually, I'm not leaving just yet.
3 Actually, I found it extremely depressing.
4 Actually, I can't swim.
5 Actually, he discovered the effects by accident.
6 Actually, I heard he only got the job . . .
Sentences 1, 2, 5, 6

2
1 Actually 2 Both 3 and indeed
4 Actually 5 Both 6 Both

18 Exemplification and summation: *For example, for instance, all in all, in short*

1
1	Incorrect	As a result
2	Correct	
3	Incorrect	For instance / for example
4	Correct	
5	Correct	
6	Incorrect	Anyway / In any case

2
1–All in all–C
2–In short–B
3–All in all–A
4–In short–D
5–In short–E

3
1 b–a; a; For instance
2 b–a; a; In short
3 a–b; b; For example
4 a–b; b; All in all
5 a–b; b; For example

19 Organisation and narrative linkers: *Firstly, at first; finally, at last*; etc.

1
1 At first I didn't enjoy the work.
2 Firstly, she is extremely well qualified.
3 Firstly, you haven't tightened these screws.
4 At first they'll only be available in the London stores, . . .
5 Firstly, it should have invested in new technology.
6 At first it was thought that chemical agents were responsible.

2
1 Firstly/First of all 2 In the end
3 Secondly 4 At first 5 At the start 6 At the end 7 Finally
8 At last

20 Addition: *In addition to, besides, as well as* (sample answers)

1
1 He owns a flat in London in addition to his castles . . .
2 As well as checking the students' grammar . . .
3 Besides her reputation as a novelist . . .
4 You may take one more course in addition to the courses . . .
5 As well as giving you an X-ray . . .
6 . . . pop music as well as from classical music.
7 . . . enemies as well as helpful to our friends.
8 . . . experience besides the job you had in Hong Kong?
9 . . . expenditure in addition to the £7.5 billion . . .

2
1 (a) John got US dollars for the journey. In addition, he got travellers' cheques.
(b) John got US dollars for the journey in addition to travellers' cheques.
2 (a) She is efficient. She is extremely clever as well.
(b) She is efficient as well as extremely clever.
3 (a) In addition to courses in computing, a business course is on offer.
(b) There are courses in computing. In addition, a business course is on offer.
4 (a) The exhibition contained oil paintings as well as some water-colours.
(b) The exhibition contained oil paintings. It showed some water-colours as well.
5 (a) We shall provide hotel accommodation. In addition, we shall cover travel expenses.
(b) In addition to hotel accommodation, we shall cover travel expenses.

6 (a) He is endangering his own life. He is putting others in danger as well.
   (b) As well as endangering his own life, he is putting others in danger.

21 Contrast: *In spite of / despite*; versus *although* (*In spite of* can be used instead of *despite* in these sentences.)

1
1 He was never satisfied, despite being one of the richest men in the world.
2 We arrived on time, despite the heavy traffic on the motorway.
3 Despite losing two early goals, our team won comfortably in the end.
4 Despite our present economic difficulties, the company should recover next year.
5 Despite receiving death threats, the police chief fought against the Mafia.
6 Despite widespread prejudice against women, she became president of the company.
7 Despite working hard all his life, Joe did not become wealthy.
8 Despite the severity of the earthquake, relatively few buildings were damaged.
9 Despite having just had a baby, Jill is back at work.

2
1 in spite of; although
2 Although; although
3 despite; although
4 Despite; in spite of

22 Reason: *Because of* (versus *because*)

1
1 He had a strict upbringing because of his parents' religious beliefs.
2 He won a scholarship to a famous school because of his abilities in maths and sport.
3 The other boys teased him because of his strange regional accent.
4 He wanted to join the army because of a desire for adventure.
5 At first the army would not take him because of his age.
6 He became a successful commander because of his qualities of leadership.
7 He was given many medals because of bravery in battle.
8 He retired from the army at 45 because of ill-health.

2
1 Many students failed because the exam was so difficult.
2 Because of her hard work, Joan soon became indispensable to the company.
3 Tim has to go to the dentist because he has an infected tooth.
4 Everyone in the class was punished because Joy behaved foolishly.
5 The motorist was fined £100 because of his dangerous driving.
6 Alice has joined a choir because she loves singing.

3
1 Because   2 because of; because
3 because of; because

23 Reason: *As a result of / because of; owing to / due to*

1
1 Because of   2 as a result of   3 as a result of   4 Because of   5 as a result of   6 because of   7 because of   8 as a result of   9 As a result of   10 Because of   11 as a result of

2
1 Owing to   2 due to   3 owing to   4 due to   5 owing to   6 owing to

24 Clarification: *Namely, i.e., for example / e.g., such as, including, especially*

1
1 ... England, namely Eton.
2 ..., i.e. the cousin who had helped her ...
3 ..., namely Buenos Aires and Rio de Janeiro.
4 ..., namely the Tranox 486.
5 ..., i.e. a present he had no use for whatsoever.
6 ..., namely myself.
7 ..., i.e. planets with oxygen and water.

2
1 such as   2 for example   3 i.e.
4 such as   5 such as   6 including
7 namely   8 especially   9 i.e.
10 namely

25 Time: *During* (versus *while* and *meanwhile*)

1
1 We hope you enjoy yourselves during your stay with us.
2 (while)
3 One of our players was injured during the match and had to leave the field.
4 John was comforted by many expressions of sympathy during his long illness.
5 I'll phone my wife during the coffee break.
6 (while)

2
1 during   2 while   3 during
4 while   5 While   6 during
7 while   8 while   9 During

3
1 Meanwhile   2 during
3 Meanwhile   4 while
5 Meanwhile

26 Review 1: Linkers from sections 1 and 2

1
1 (b)   2 (a)   3 (c)   4 (a)   5 (c)
6 (a)   7 (c)   8 (a)   9 (c)   10 (a)
11 (c)   12 (a)   13 (c)

2
1 At first   2 but   3 so   4 Firstly
5 The thing is   6 As a matter of fact
7 Whereas   8 By the way
9 because   10 Anyway
11 provided   12 In other words
13 For example   14 Alternatively
15 In addition   16 in case   17 In fact   18 On the contrary   19 All in all

27 Review 2: Linkers from sections 2 and 3

1
1 At last   2 During   3 Incidentally
4 namely   5 In spite of
6 including   7 i.e.   8 but in fact
9 In the end   10 Indeed
11 However   12 For example
13 owing to   14 Moreover   15 due to   16 as well as   17 In addition to
18 For instance   19 hence
20 such as   21 especially
22 however   23 at least   24 e.g.
25 Nevertheless   26 therefore

2
1 namely   2 and indeed   3 By contrast   4 However   5 or rather
6 First of all   7 Actually
8 Anyway   9 Secondly   10 i.e.
11 In other words   12 Actually
13 namely   14 such as   15 The thing is   16 Hence   17 Otherwise
18 Conversely   19 Consequently
20 in other words

28 Review 3: Linkers from all sections

1
1 (a)   2 (c)   3 (d)   4 (b)
5 (a)   6 (d)   7 (a)   8 (a)
9 (d)   10 (d)   11 (d)   12 (a)
13 (d)   14 (a)   15 (d)